T0021117

The Land Before Time Management

ADHDINOS

based on the viral webcomic

The Land Before Time Management

ADHDINOS

Ryan Keats

UNION
SQUARE
& CO.

NEW YORK

UNION
SQUARE
& CO.

NEW YORK

UNION SQUARE & CO. and the distinctive Union Square & Co. logo
are trademarks of Sterling Publishing Co., Inc.

Union Square & Co., LLC, is a subsidiary of Sterling Publishing Co., Inc.

©2023 Ryan Keats

All rights reserved. No part of this publication may be reproduced,
stored in a retrieval system, or transmitted in any form or by any means
(including electronic, mechanical, photocopying, recording, or otherwise)
without prior written permission from the publisher.

ISBN 978-1-4549-5057-8 (hardcover)
ISBN 978-1-4549-5058-5 (e-book)

For information about custom editions, special sales,
and premium purchases, please contact
specialsales@unionsquareandco.com.

Printed in China

2 4 6 8 10 9 7 5 3 1

unionsquareandco.com

To Mom, Dad, and Jackie

The best supports a Dino could ask for
And to everyone trying their best—
that's all anyone can ever ask of you

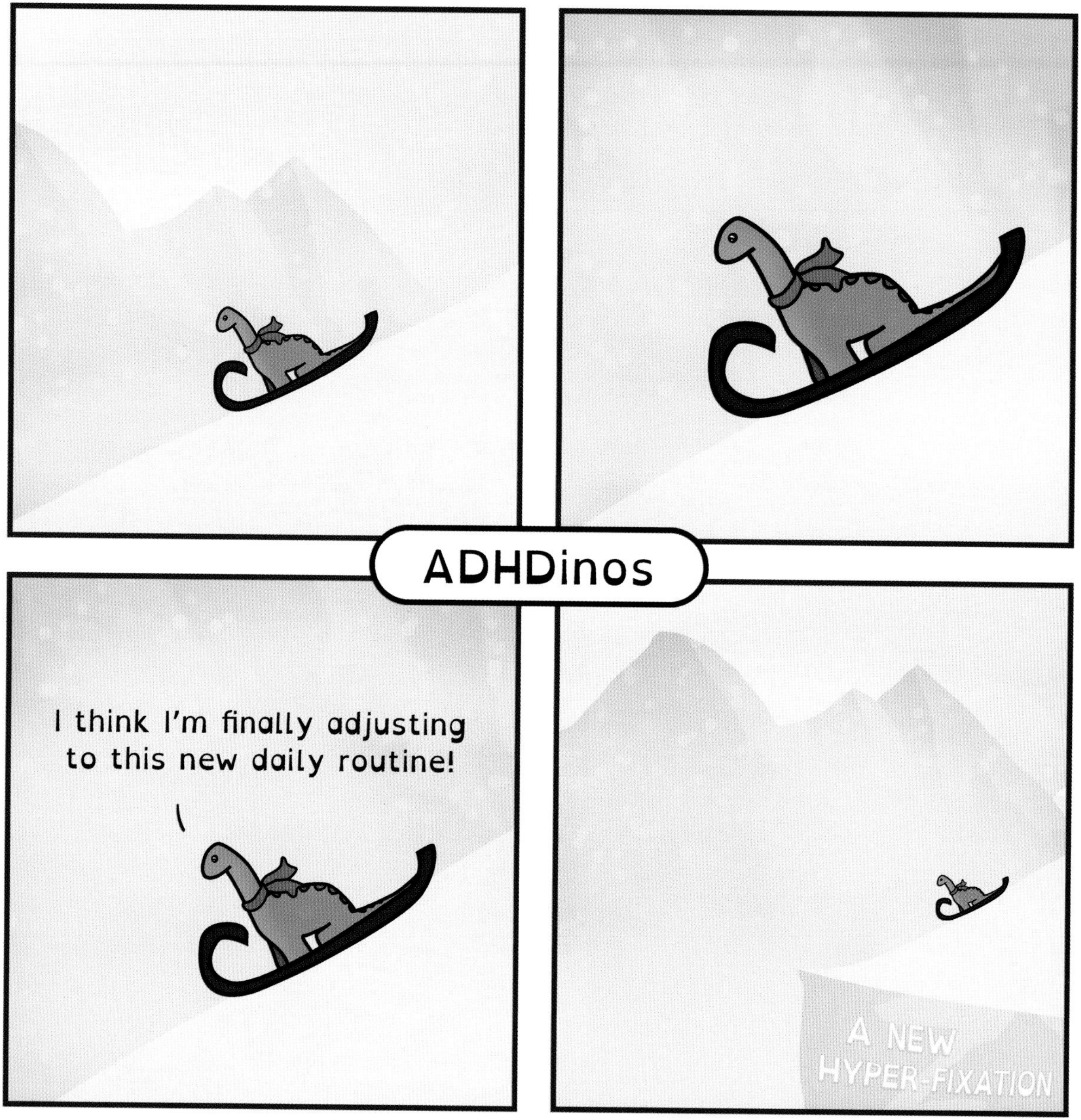
ADHDinos
I think I'm finally adjusting to this new daily routine!
A NEW HYPER-FIXATION

Things I Want to Address

* Through these comics, I am doing my best to work through ADHD and the things I have encountered as a result of it.

* Each comic is a small portion of a much bigger experience.

* I only make comics that directly apply to my experience, so I cannot capture ADHD as a whole.

* I'm not a medical professional. If you believe you may have ADHD and wish to pursue a diagnosis, I encourage you to seek out help through trained professionals.

* The topics within the comics apply to ADHD, but they're certainly not exclusive to it. Individuals without ADHD frequently relate to the comics and the topics they discuss. A diagnosis of ADHD is typically made in cases when a person frequently engages in behaviors that become major barriers to enjoying everyday life.

* The purpose of these comics is not to determine whether a reader does or does not have ADHD, and the comics should not be used as the basis of a diagnosis.

Introduction

Hello friend,

My name is Ryan, and I was diagnosed with ADHD at the age of twenty-two. Even though this diagnosis didn't change anything about me as a person, it definitely changed how I saw myself and how I approached many issues.

Following my diagnosis, I learned a lot about myself and ADHD. By simply having the ADHD label to go along with my questions and struggles, I found not only the answers I needed but also a considerable amount of information and support that I never knew existed.

As I learned more, I started a collection of notes. I wrote down things I struggled with and things I wanted to improve upon. On average, I still write several notes per day, but not every idea becomes a full comic.

For me, the most important part of this comic is the way it promotes visibility for these shared struggles. The most common responses to new ADHDinos comics are things like: "I feel seen," "I'm in this photo and I don't like it," and "Are you bugging my therapy sessions?" There's a strange comfort in knowing you're not the only one who struggles with something, especially after spending such a long time being convinced otherwise. The highest compliment I have received on a comic was being told that someone used it to explain an issue to a family member or friend that they had struggled to explain before. To me, that's really neat.

This book isn't just meant for people with ADHD. I believe that people without ADHD are some of the most important eyes for this information because they are the friends, family members, spouses, bosses, and whatever else of those who may just need a little bit of sympathy, support, and understanding.

I struggled with this stuff for a really long time and, truthfully, I still do. Self-improvement is hard, but I remember where I was when I started this comic and I know that I am still improving. Speaking with people at in-person events and online helps me see just how important visibility is for these issues. Above all else, this motivates me to keep making ADHDinos comics and to look for new ways to offer support. There's so much information and so many resources out there—I don't think anyone should struggle alone.

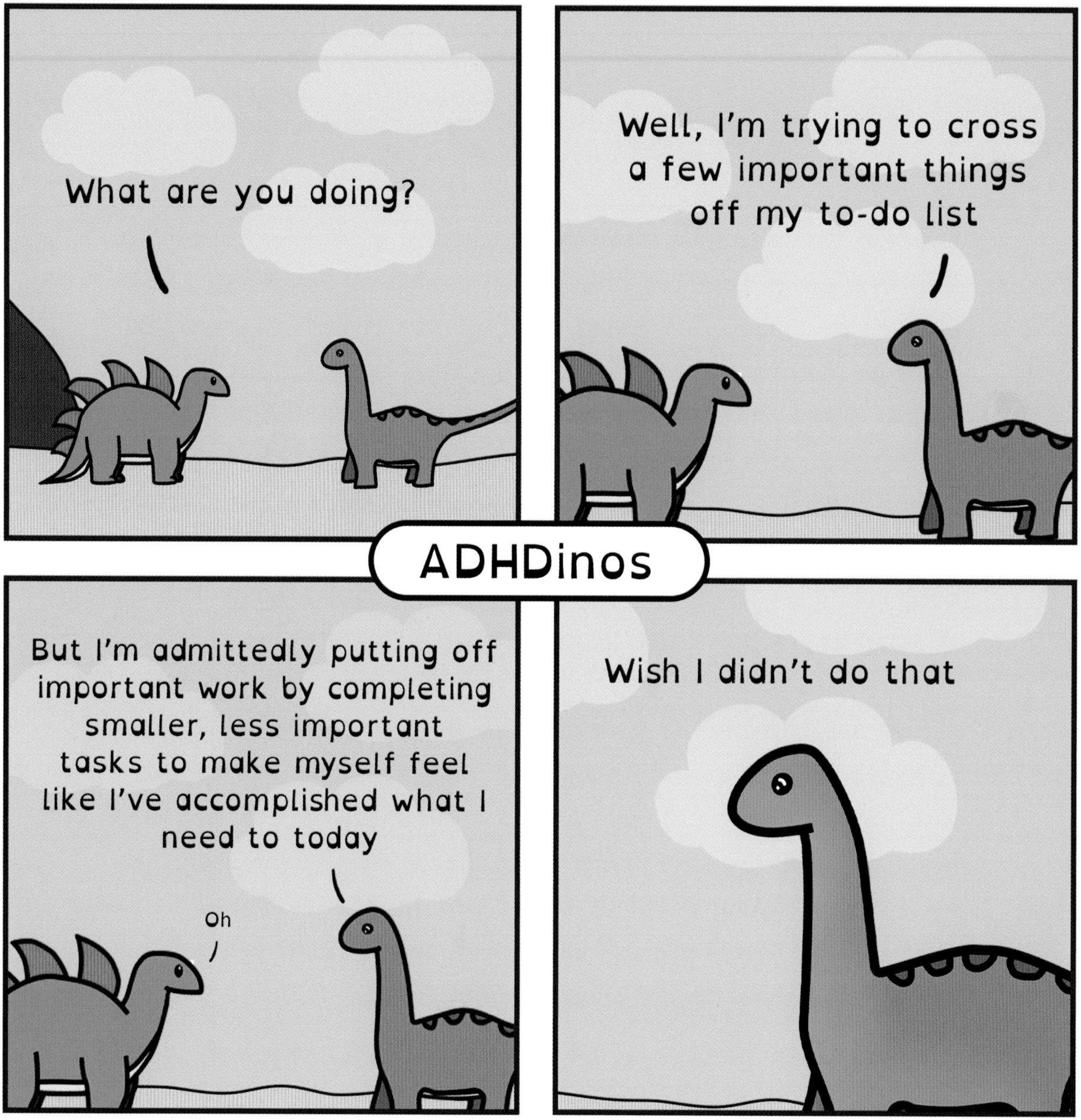
What are you doing?
Well, I'm trying to cross a few important things off my to-do list
ADHDinos
But I'm admittedly putting off important work by completing smaller, less important tasks to make myself feel like I've accomplished what I need to today
Oh
Wish I didn't do that

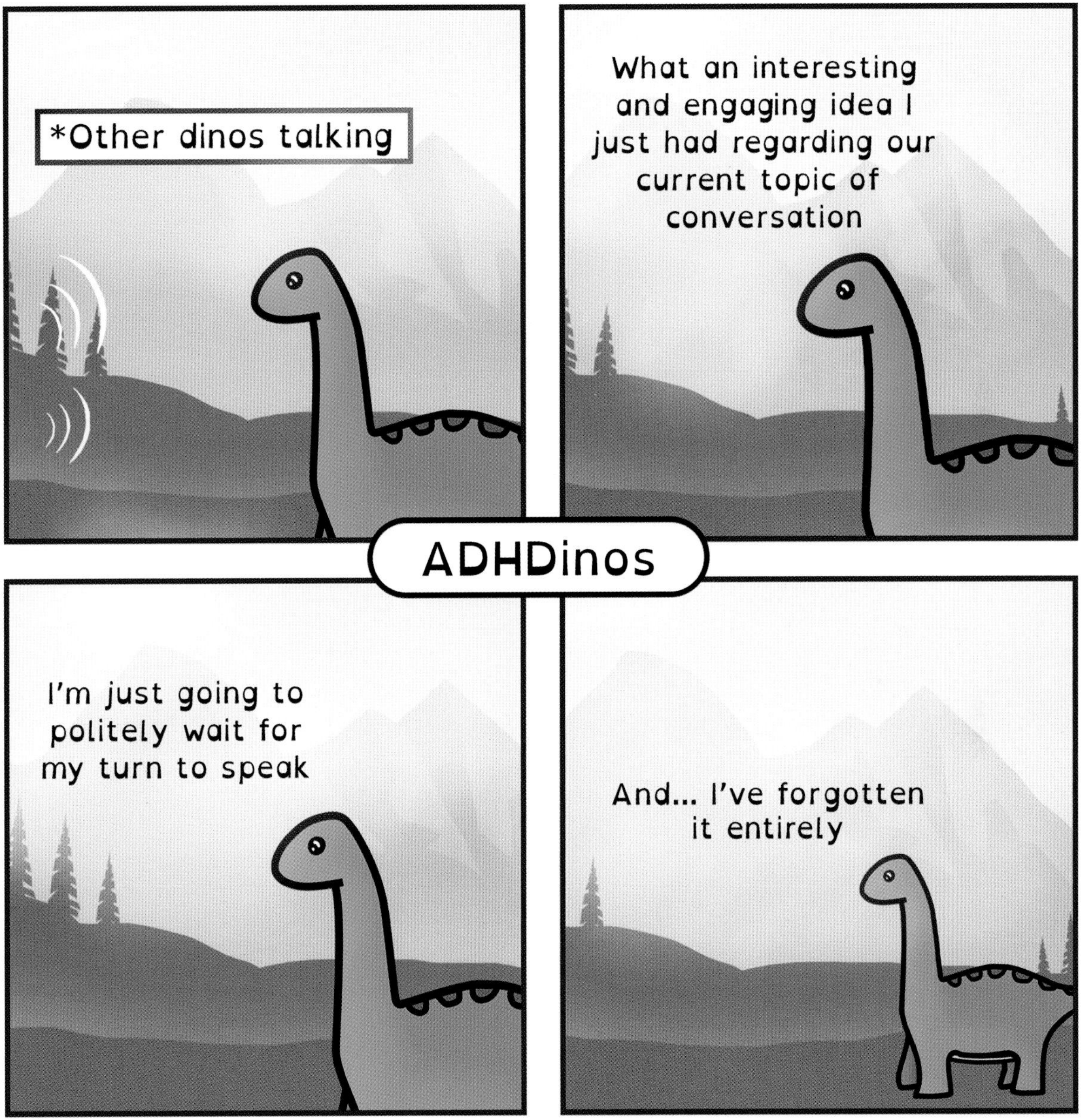
*Other dinos talking
What an interesting and engaging idea I just had regarding our current topic of conversation
ADHDinos
I'm just going to politely wait for my turn to speak
And... I've forgotten it entirely

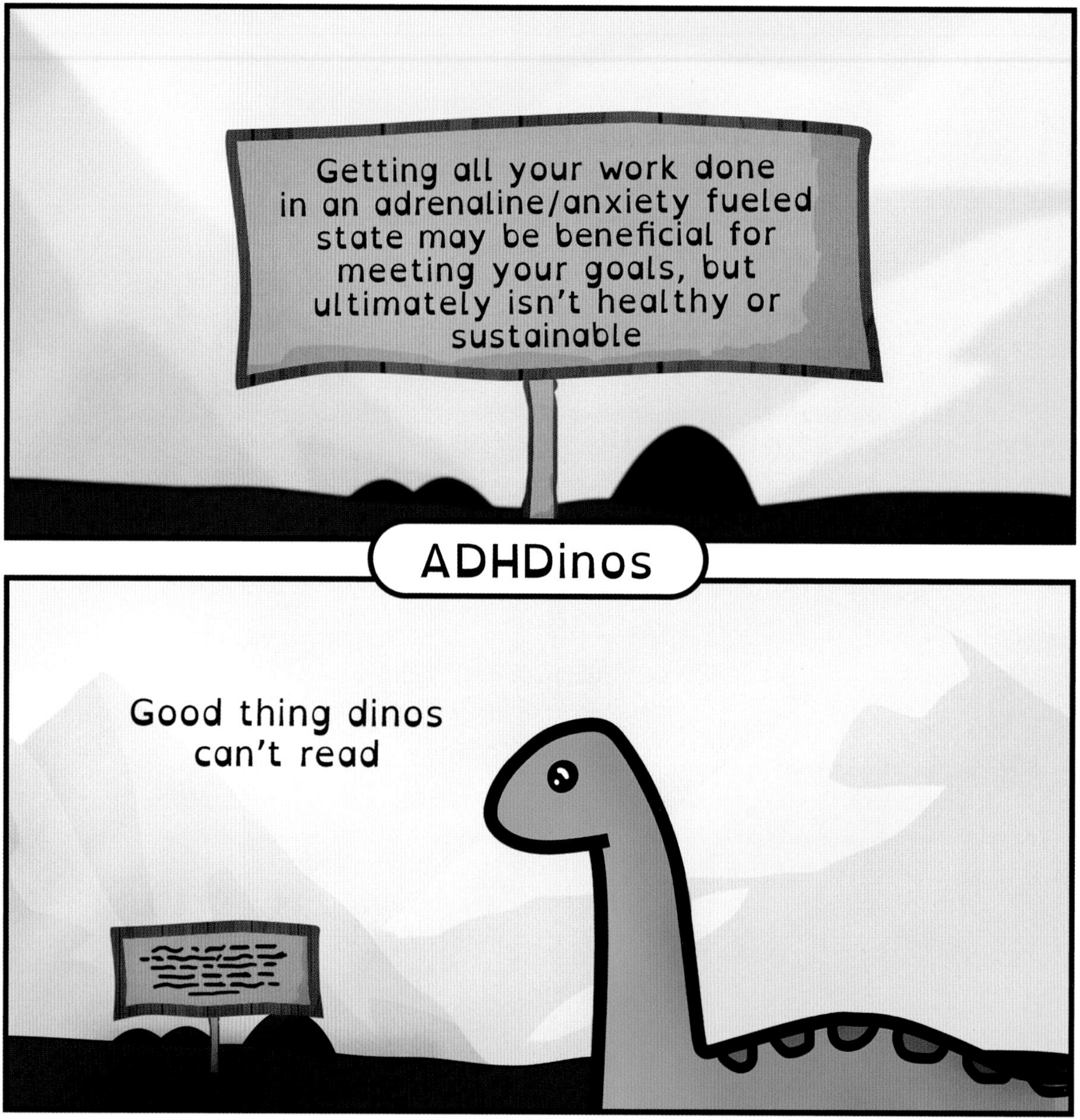
Getting all your work done in an adrenaline/anxiety fueled state may be beneficial for meeting your goals, but ultimately isn't healthy or sustainable
ADHDinos
Good thing dinos can't read

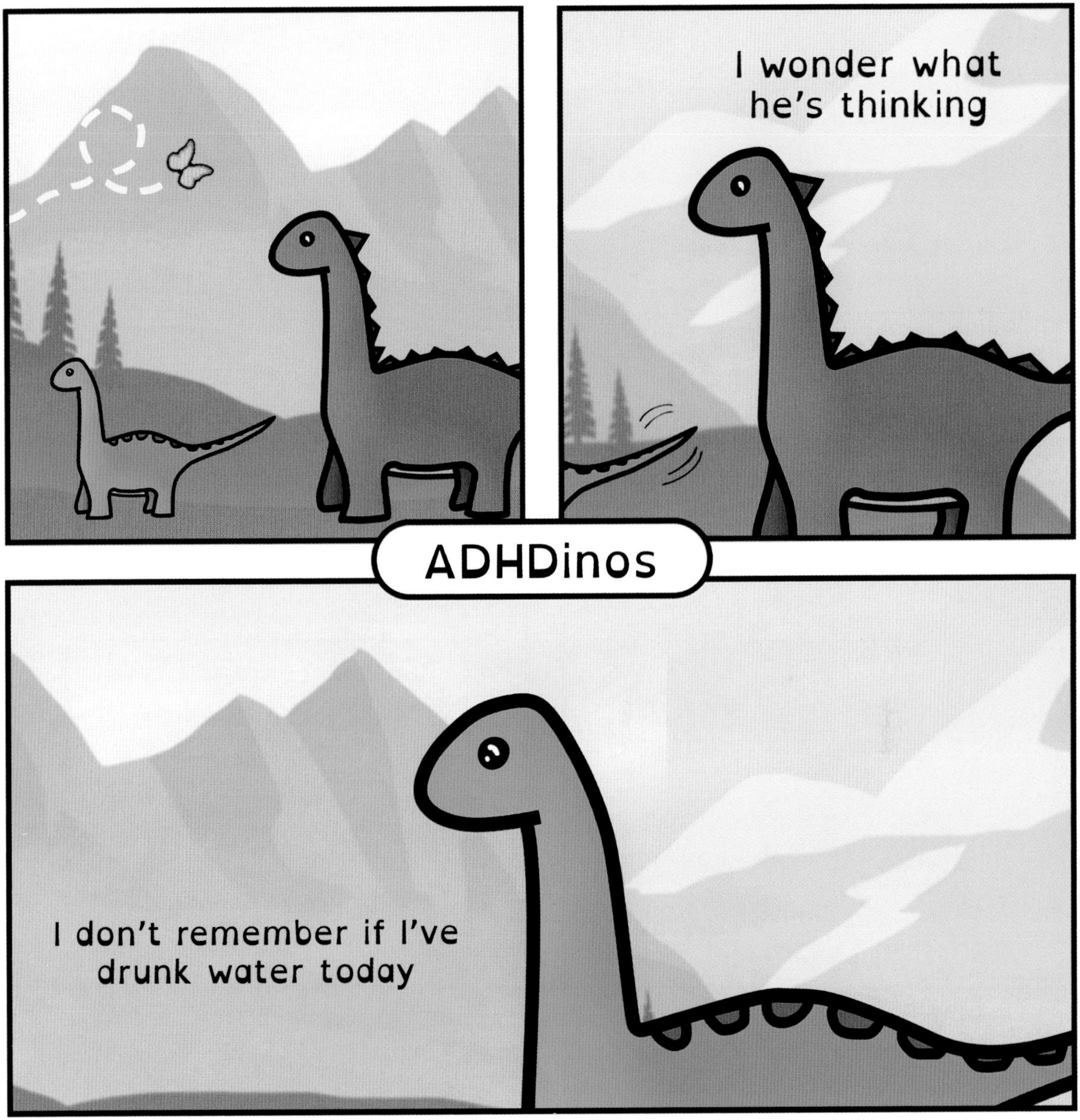
I wonder what he's thinking
ADHDinos
I don't remember if I've drunk water today

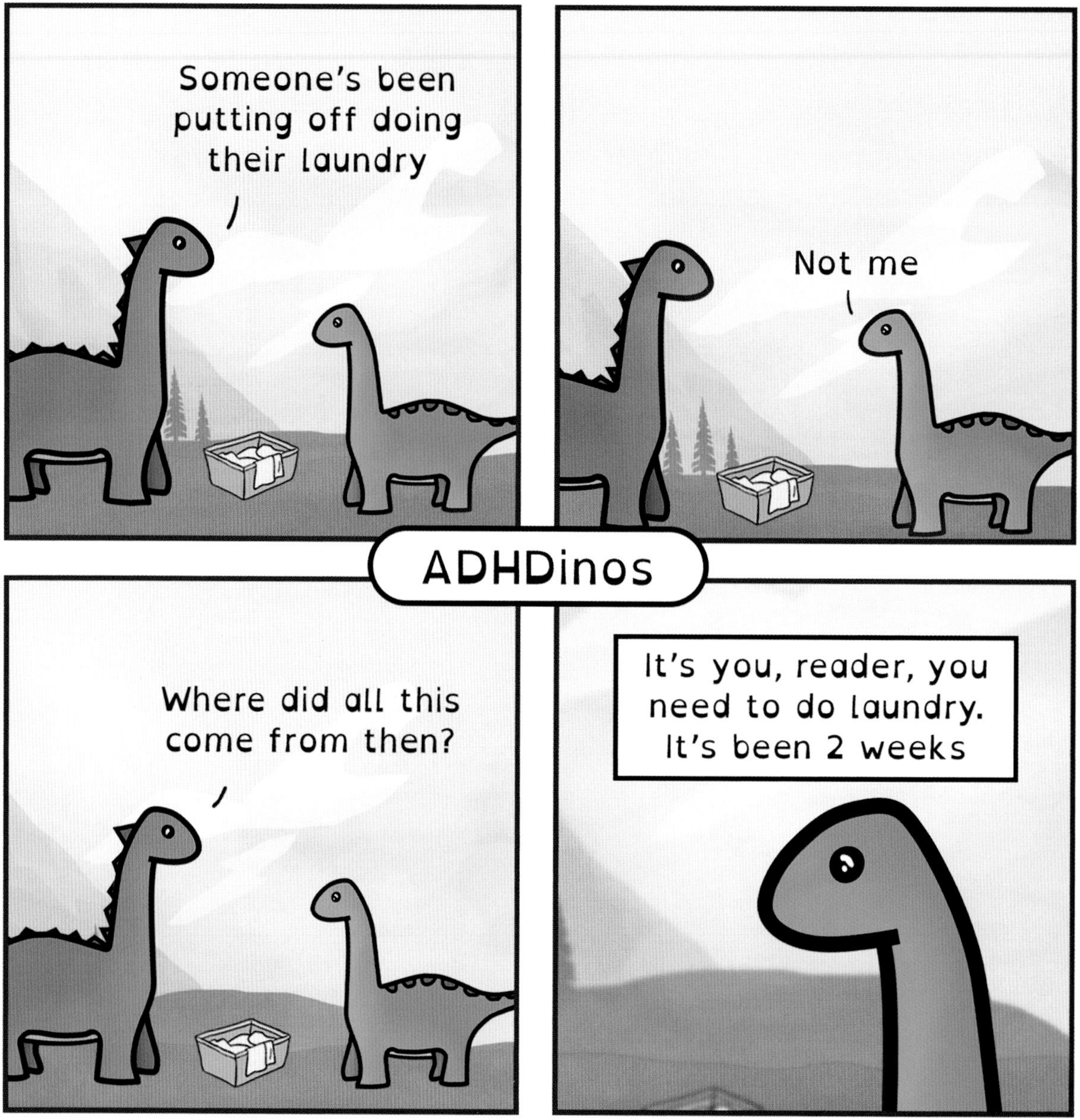
Someone's been putting off doing their laundry
Not me
ADHDinos
Where did all this come from then?
It's you, reader, you need to do laundry. It's been 2 weeks

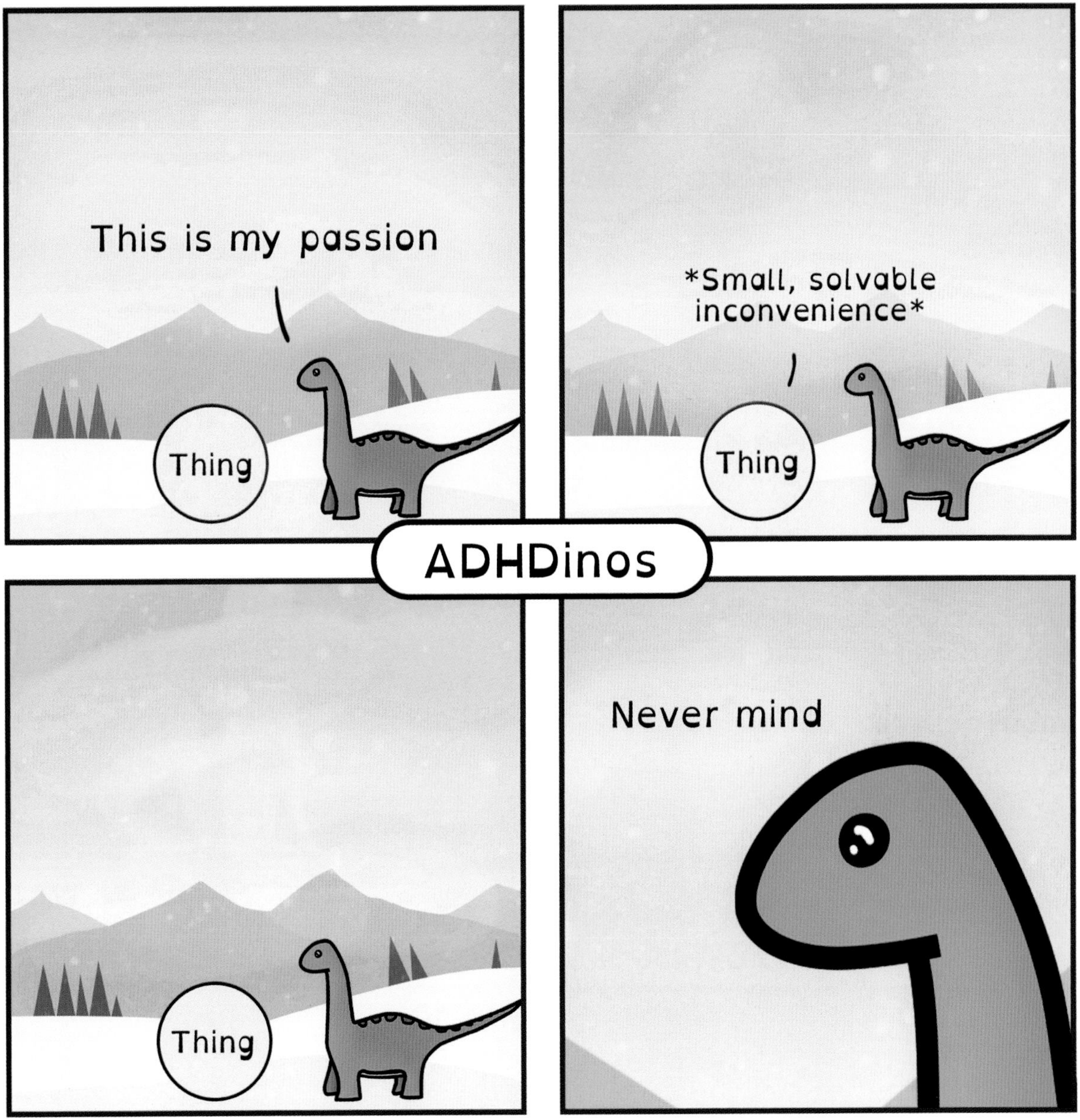
This is my passion
Thing
Small, solvable inconvenience
Thing
ADHDinos
Thing
Never mind

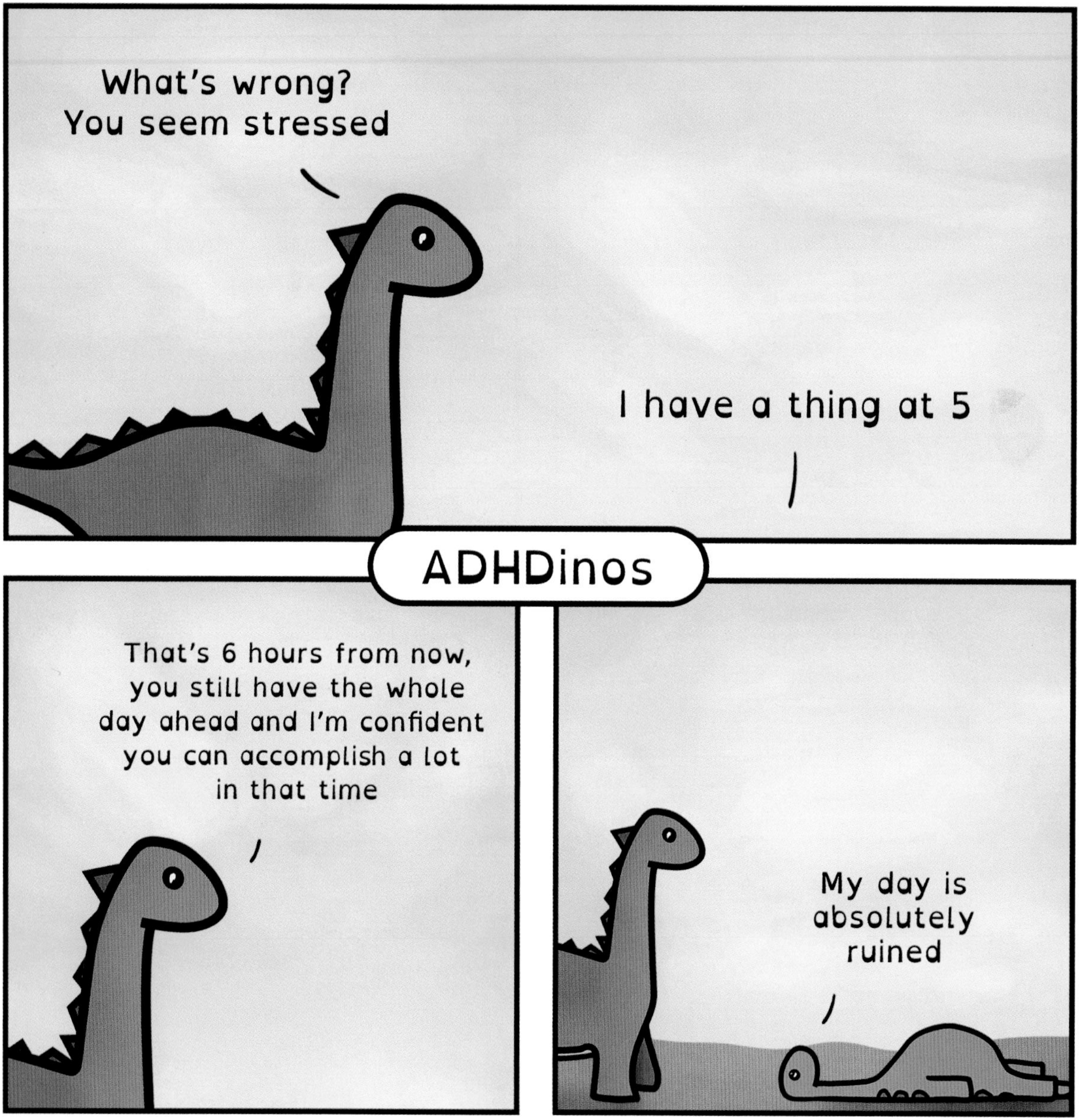

What's wrong?
You seem stressed
I have a thing at 5
ADHDinos
That's 6 hours from now, you still have the whole day ahead and I'm confident you can accomplish a lot in that time
My day is absolutely ruined

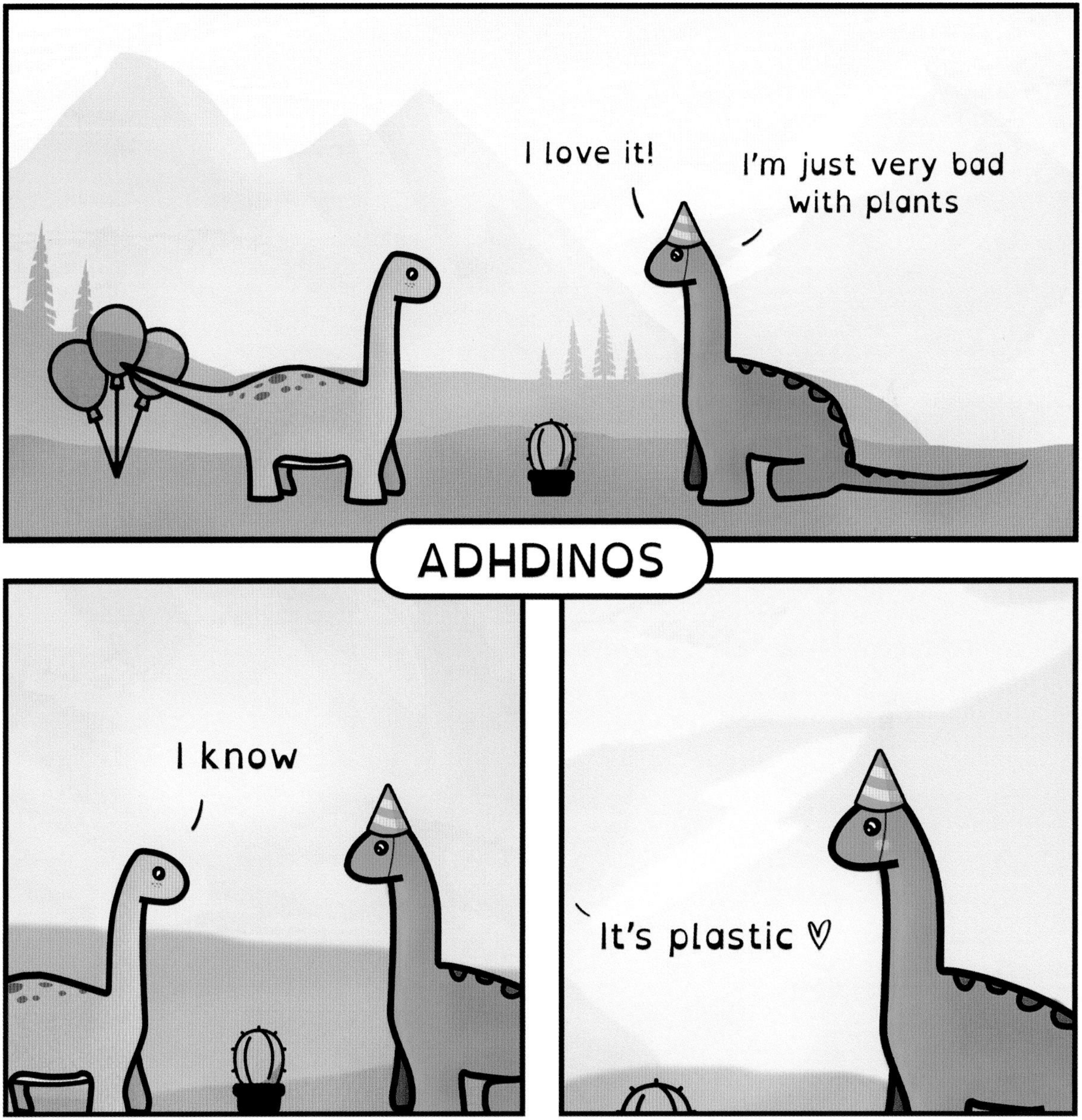
I love it!
I'm just very bad with plants
ADHDINOS
I know
It's plastic ♡

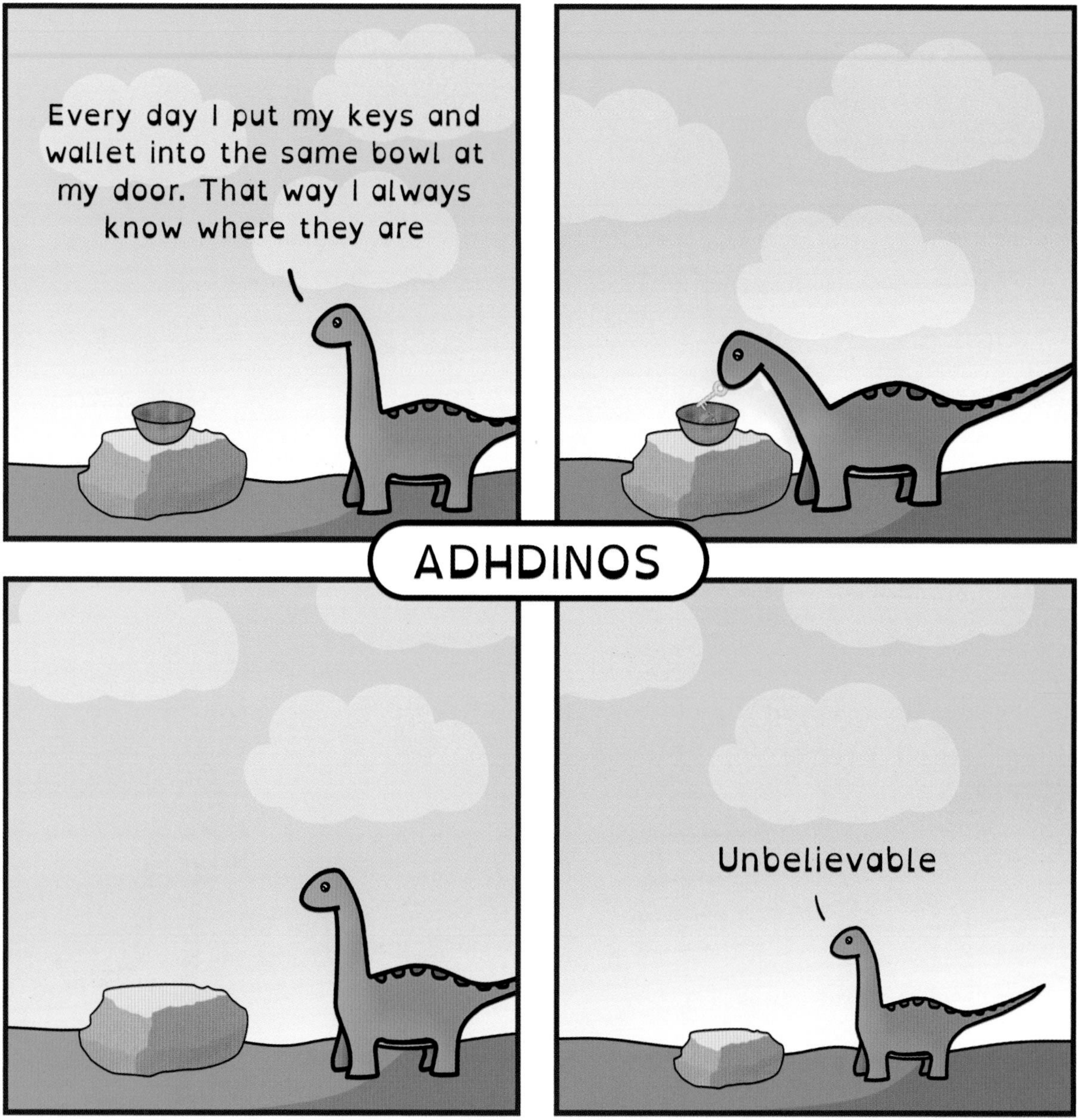
Every day I put my keys and wallet into the same bowl at my door. That way I always know where they are
ADHDINOS
Unbelievable

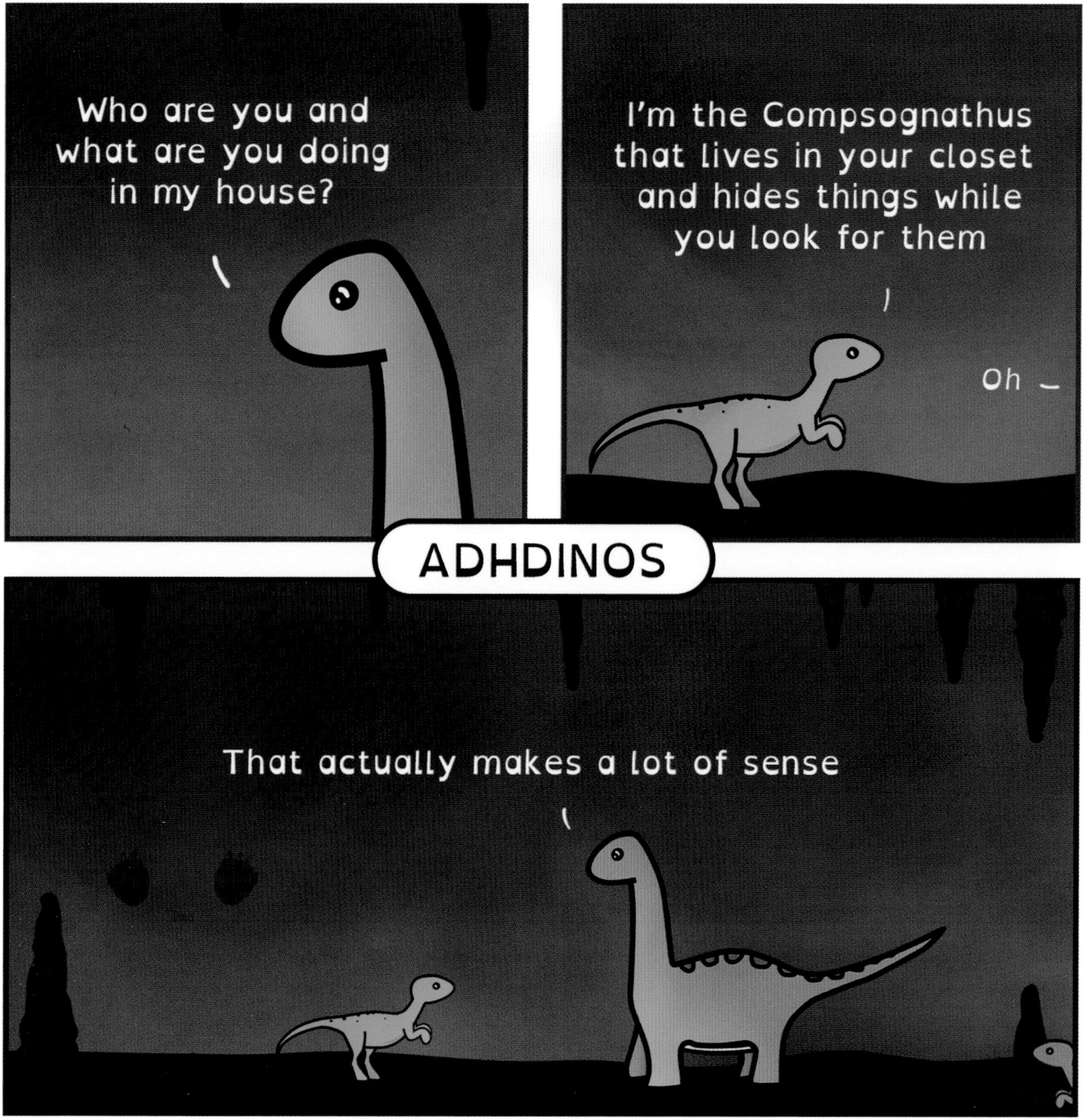
Who are you and what are you doing in my house?
I'm the Compsognathus that lives in your closet and hides things while you look for them
Oh
ADHDINOS
That actually makes a lot of sense

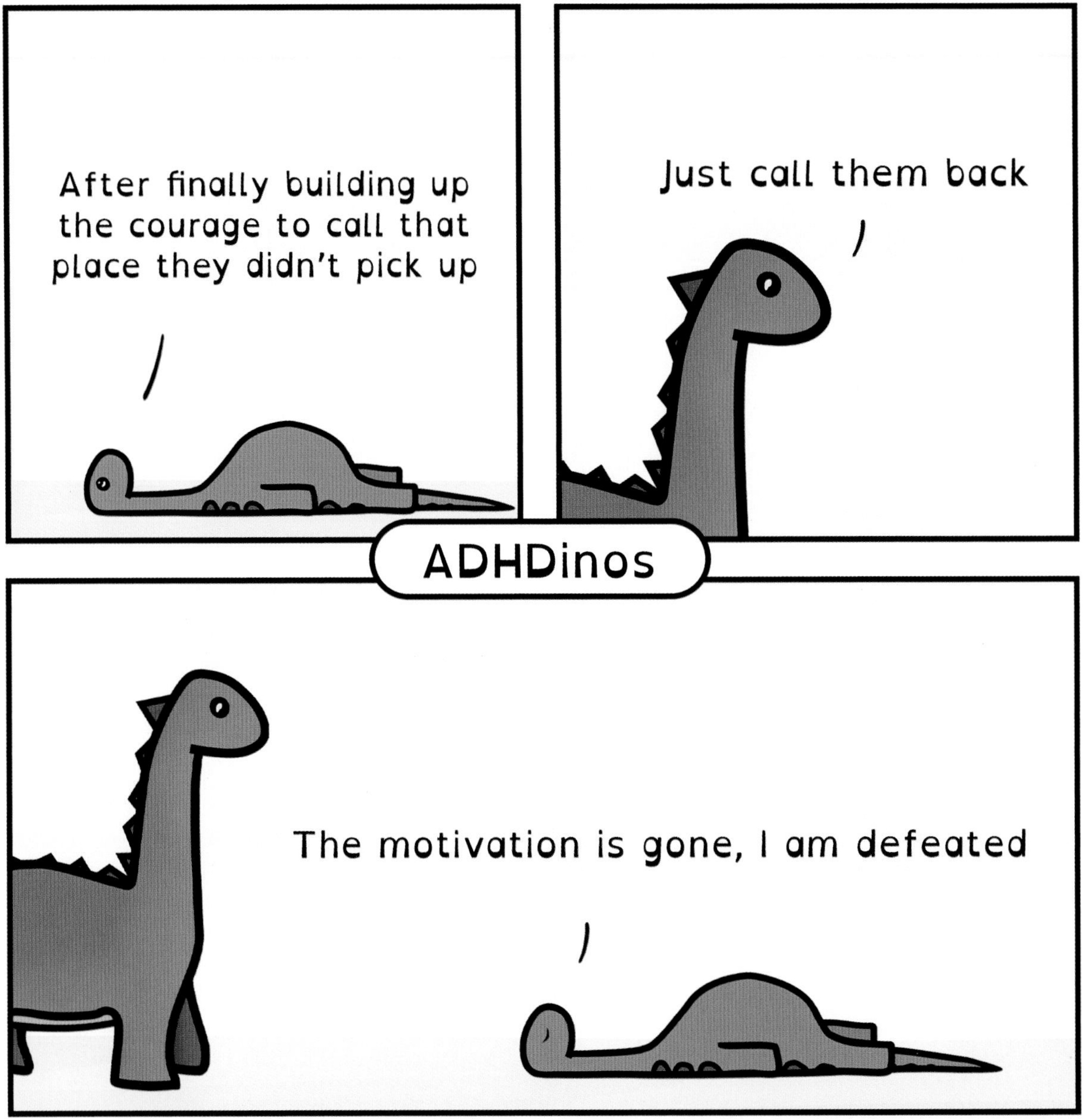
After finally building up the courage to call that place they didn't pick up
Just call them back
ADHDinos
The motivation is gone, I am defeated

"Mistakes"

Dino often feels like his own worst enemy, almost as though there's another version of himself out there who's making a bunch of mistakes on his behalf and he's entirely unaware of it. The mistakes don't feel like his fault, but the consequences are certainly his responsibility, and this other Dino sure seems to make a lot of mistakes.

From an outside perspective, mistakes are often perceived as the result of carelessness or an inattention to detail, yet those with ADHD still frequently make "careless" mistakes in the areas of their lives they care most about, usually only affecting themselves.

It can be really hard to look past shame and address an issue. Even if others are not always upset with Dino, he's often very upset with himself because the mistakes feel unnecessary.

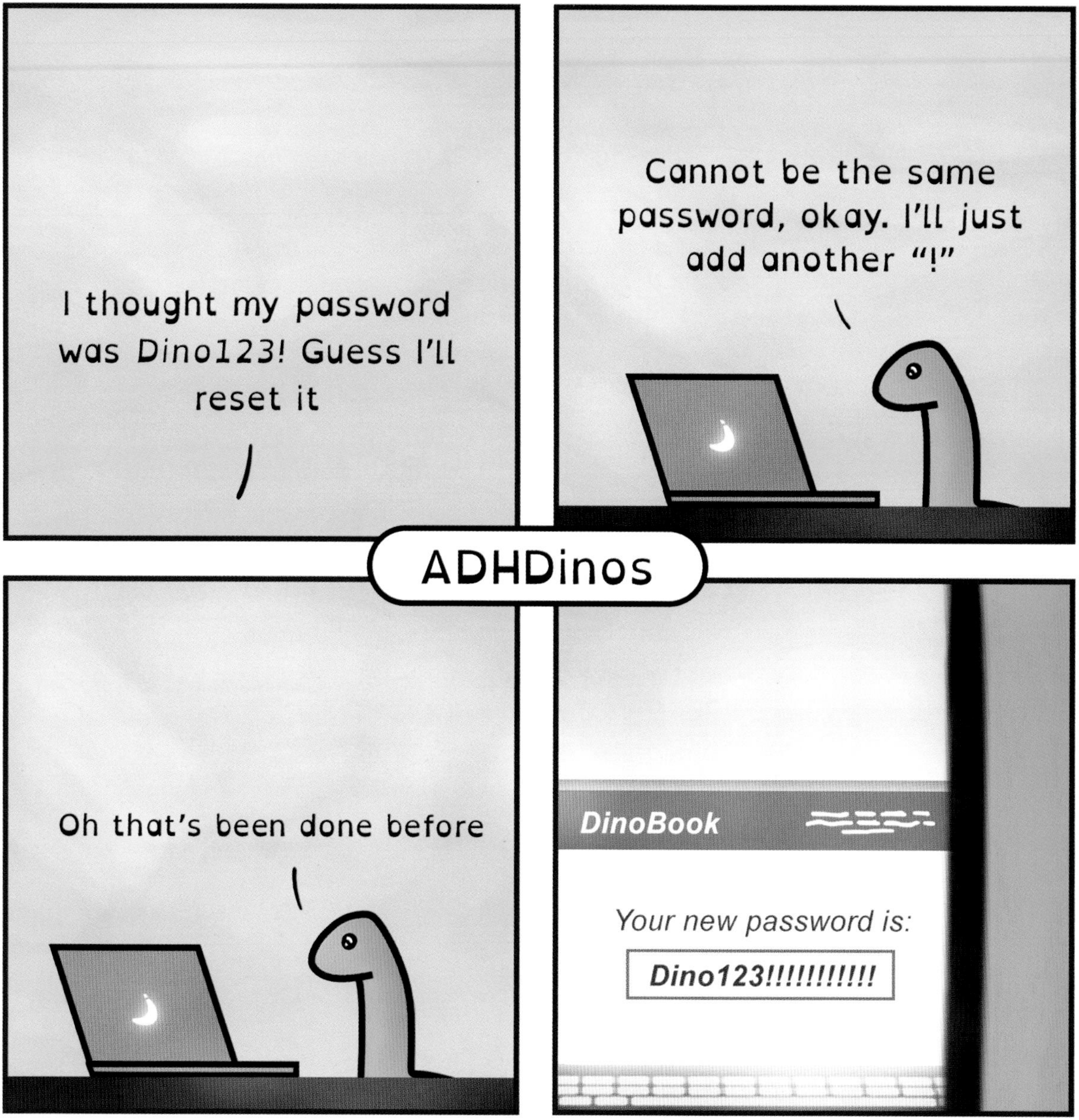
I thought my password was Dino123! Guess I'll reset it
Cannot be the same password, okay. I'll just add another "!"
ADHDinos
Oh that's been done before
DinoBook
Your new password is:
Dino123!!!!!!!!!!!

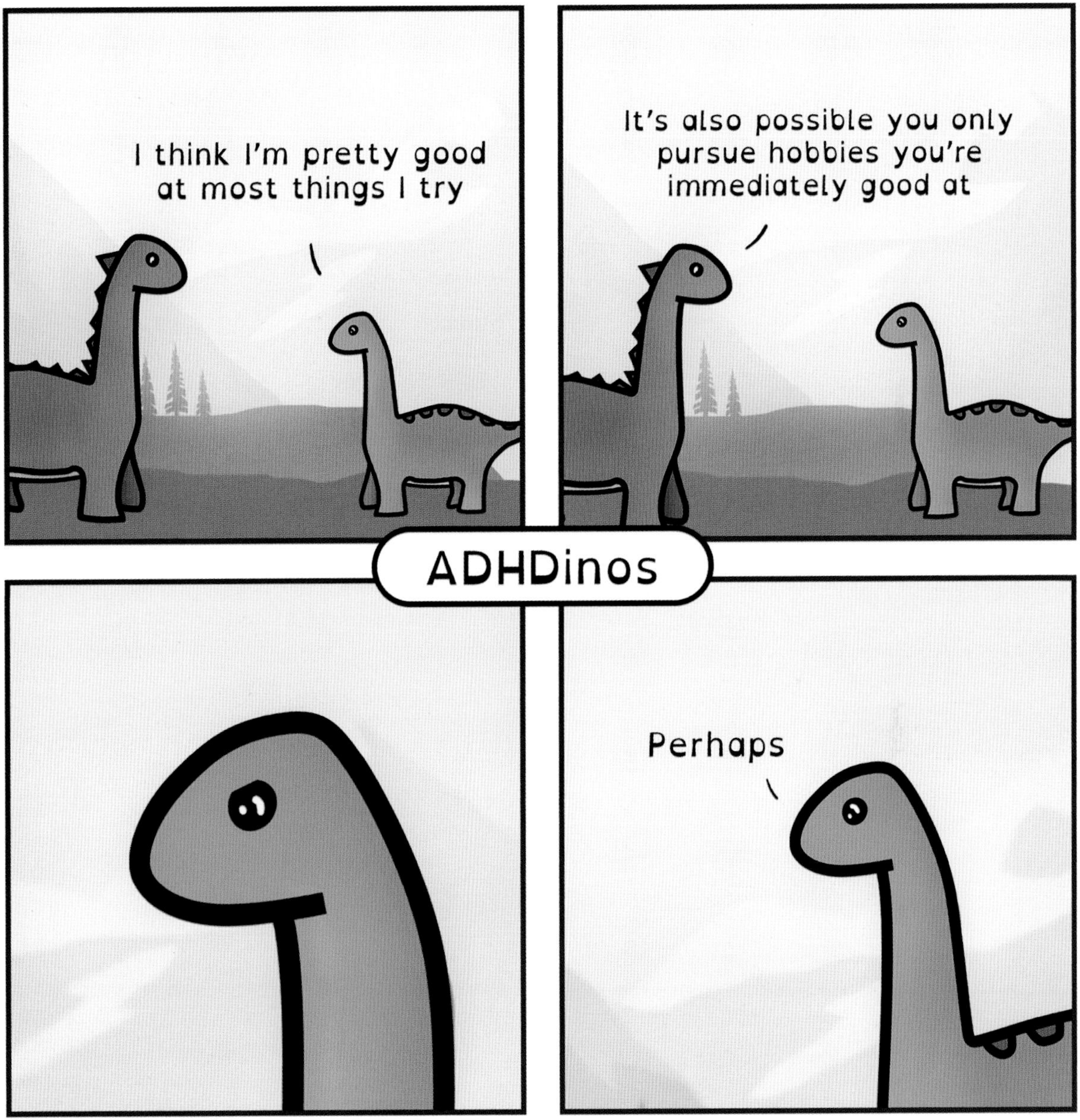
I think I'm pretty good at most things I try
It's also possible you only pursue hobbies you're immediately good at
ADHDinos
Perhaps

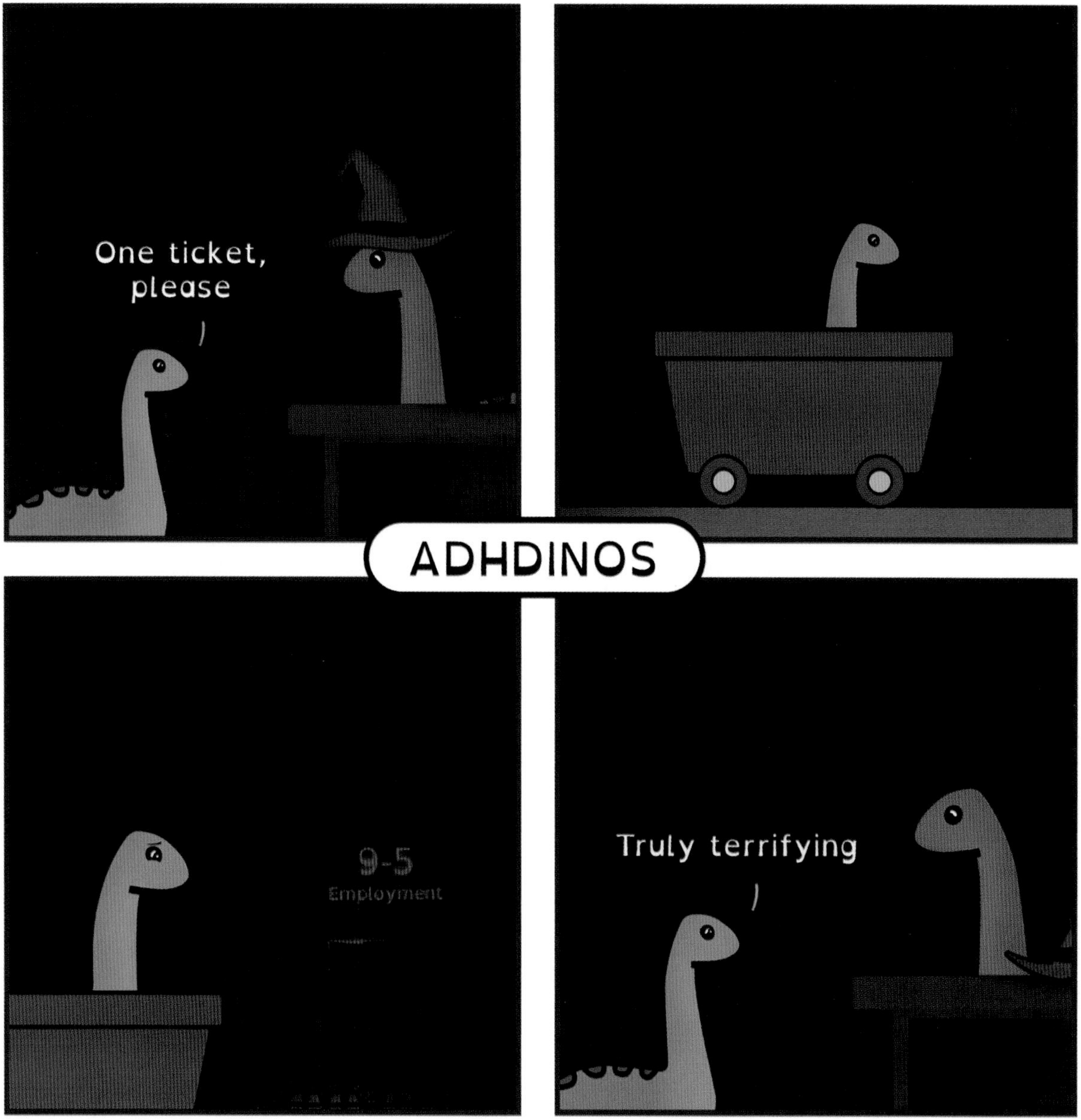
One ticket, please
ADHDINOS
9-5
Employment
Truly terrifying

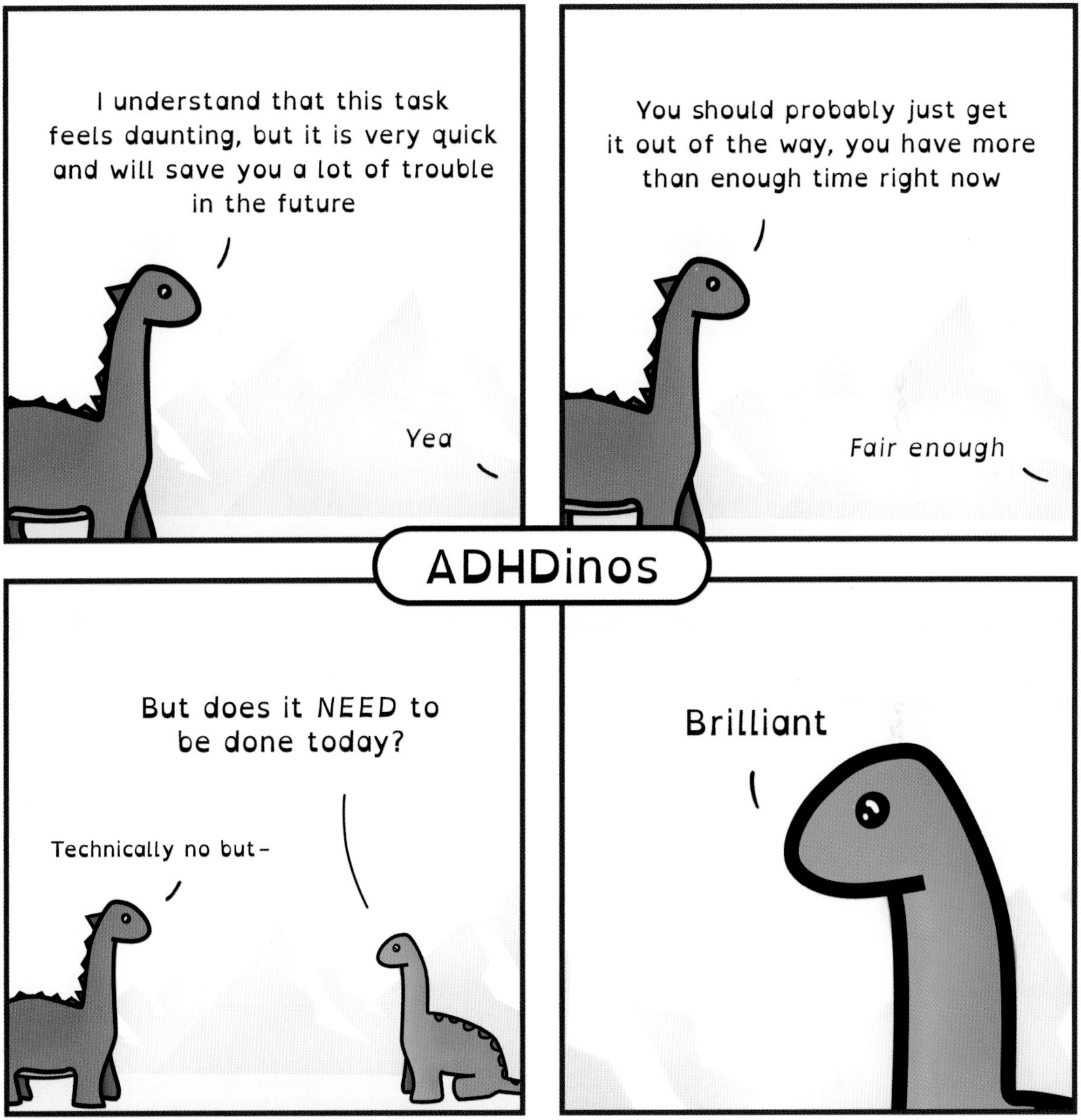
I understand that this task feels daunting, but it is very quick and will save you a lot of trouble in the future
Yea
You should probably just get it out of the way, you have more than enough time right now
Fair enough
ADHDinos
But does it *NEED* to be done today?
Technically no but-
Brilliant

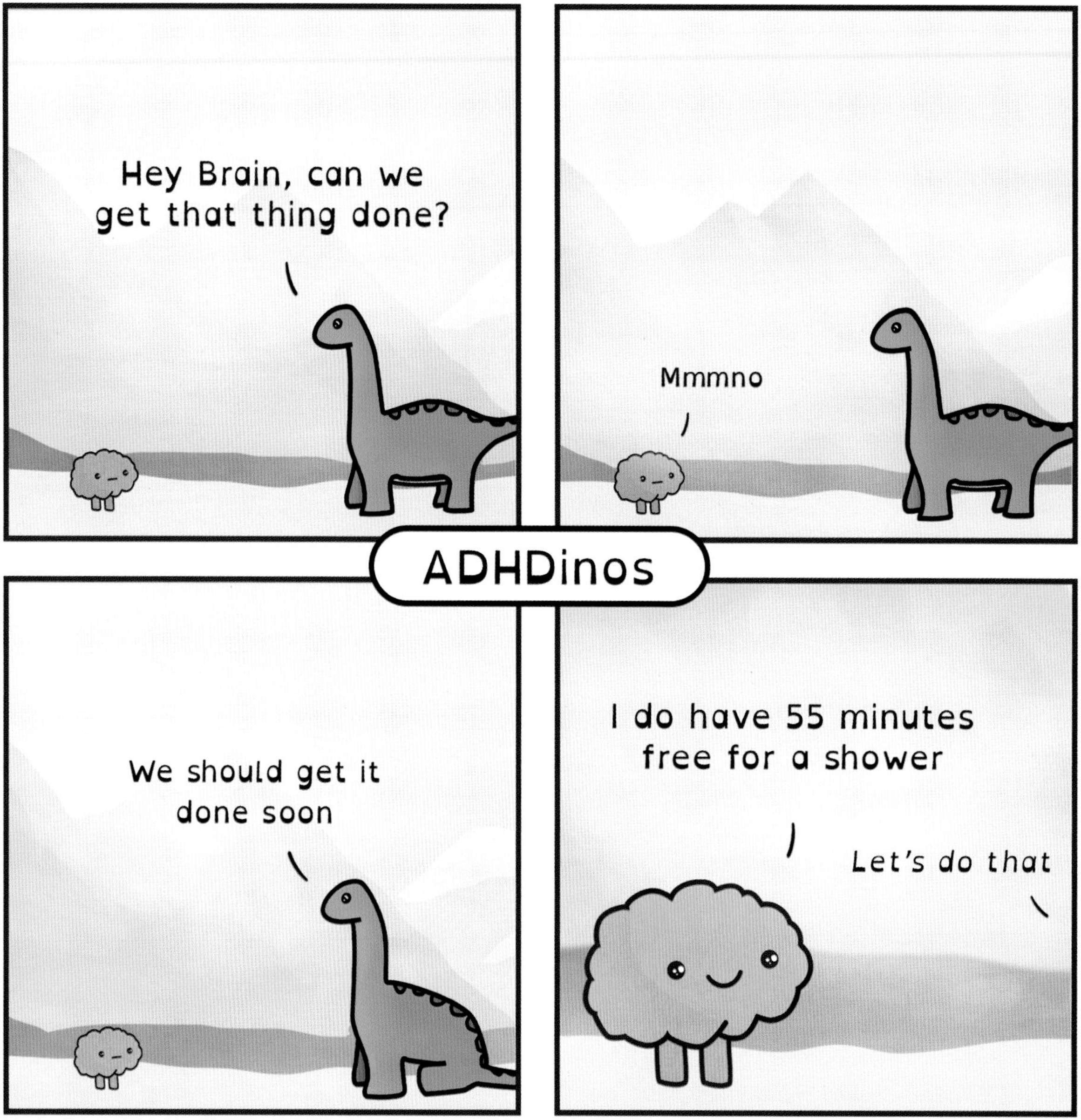
Hey Brain, can we get that thing done?
Mmmno
ADHDinos
We should get it done soon
I do have 55 minutes free for a shower
Let's do that

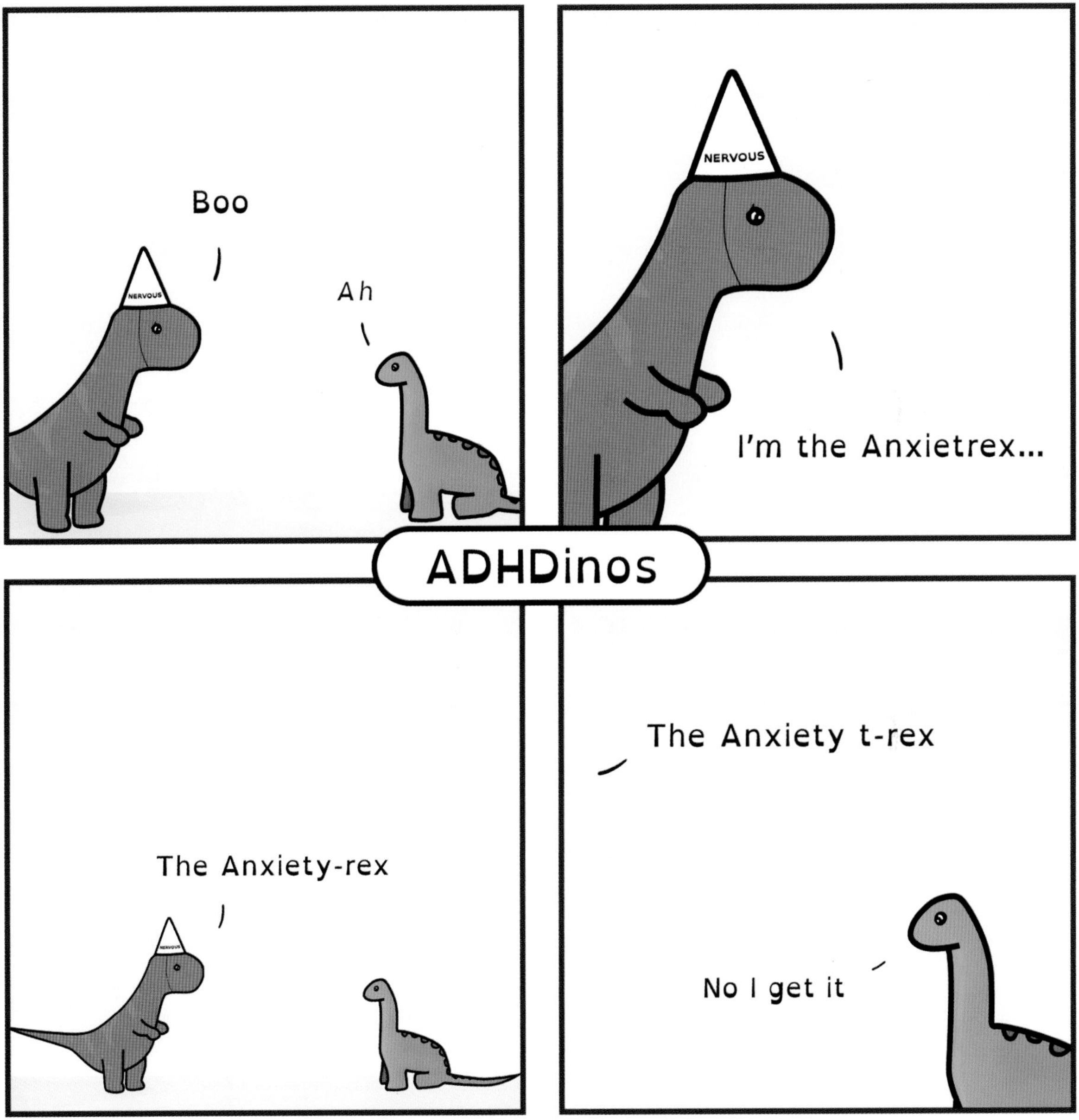
NERVOUS
Boo
Ah
NERVOUS
I'm the Anxietrex...
ADHDinos
NERVOUS
The Anxiety-rex
The Anxiety t-rex
No I get it

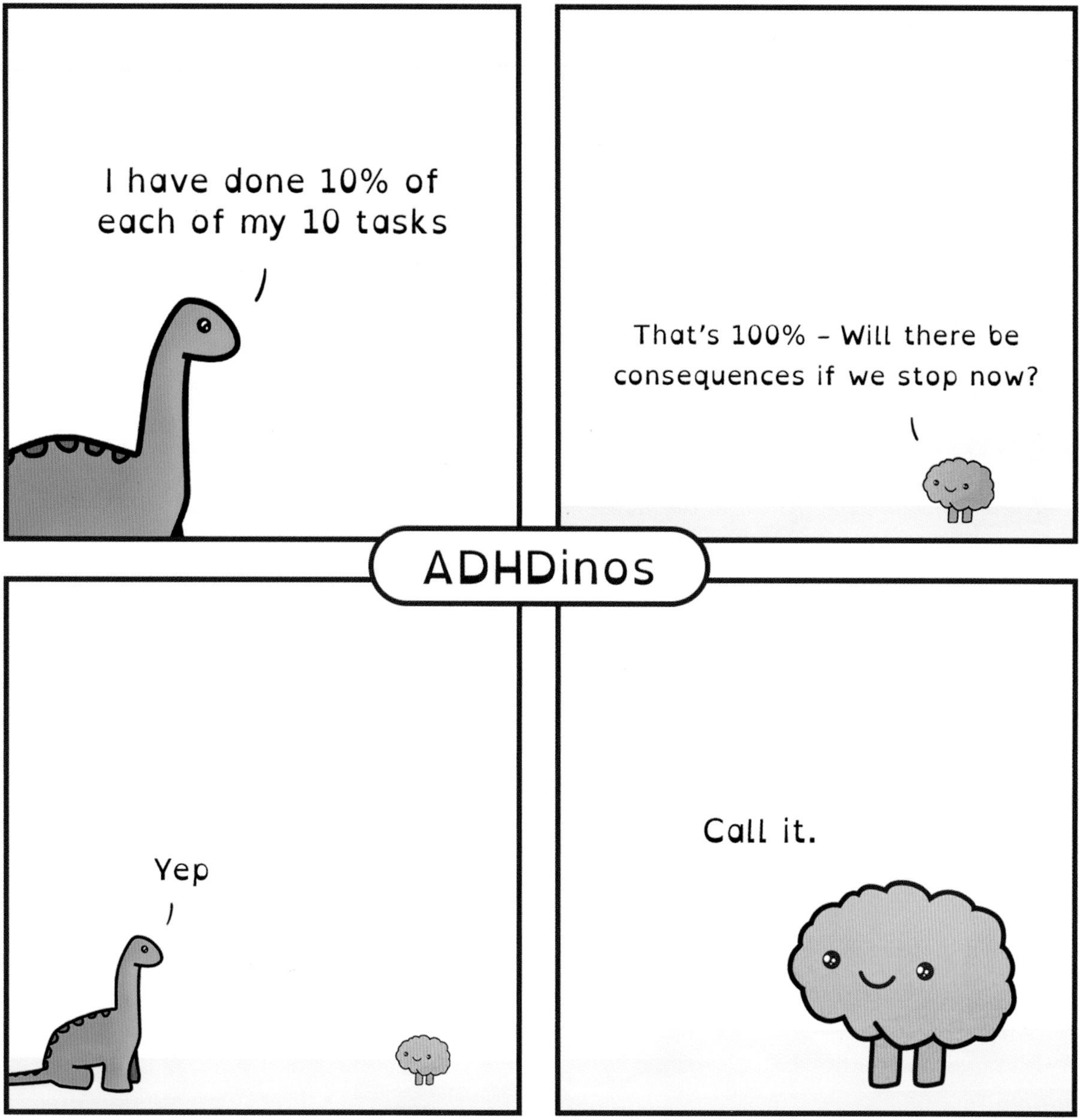
I have done 10% of each of my 10 tasks
That's 100% - Will there be consequences if we stop now?
ADHDinos
Yep
Call it.

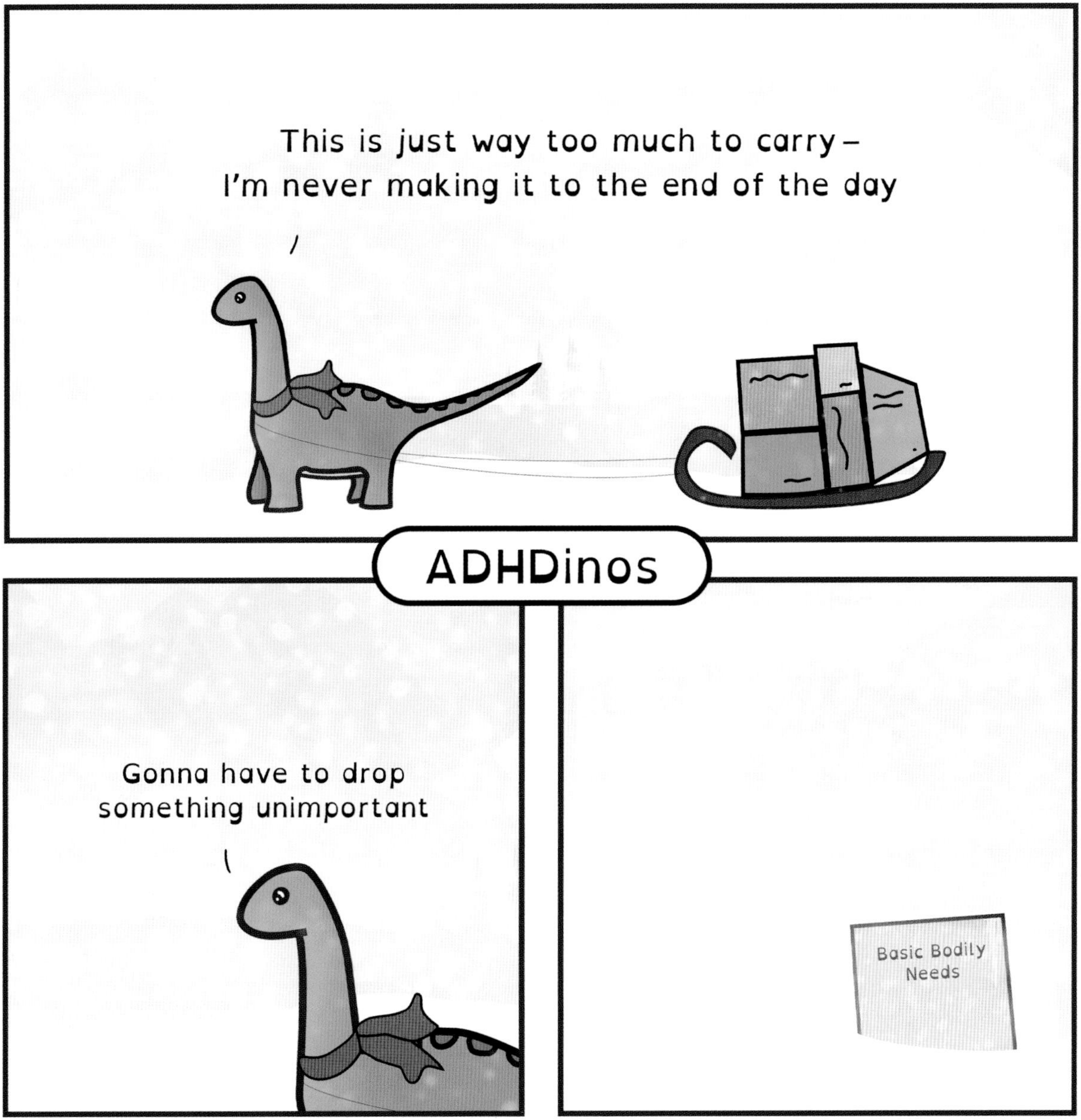
This is just way too much to carry–
I'm never making it to the end of the day
ADHDinos
Gonna have to drop
something unimportant
Basic Bodily
Needs

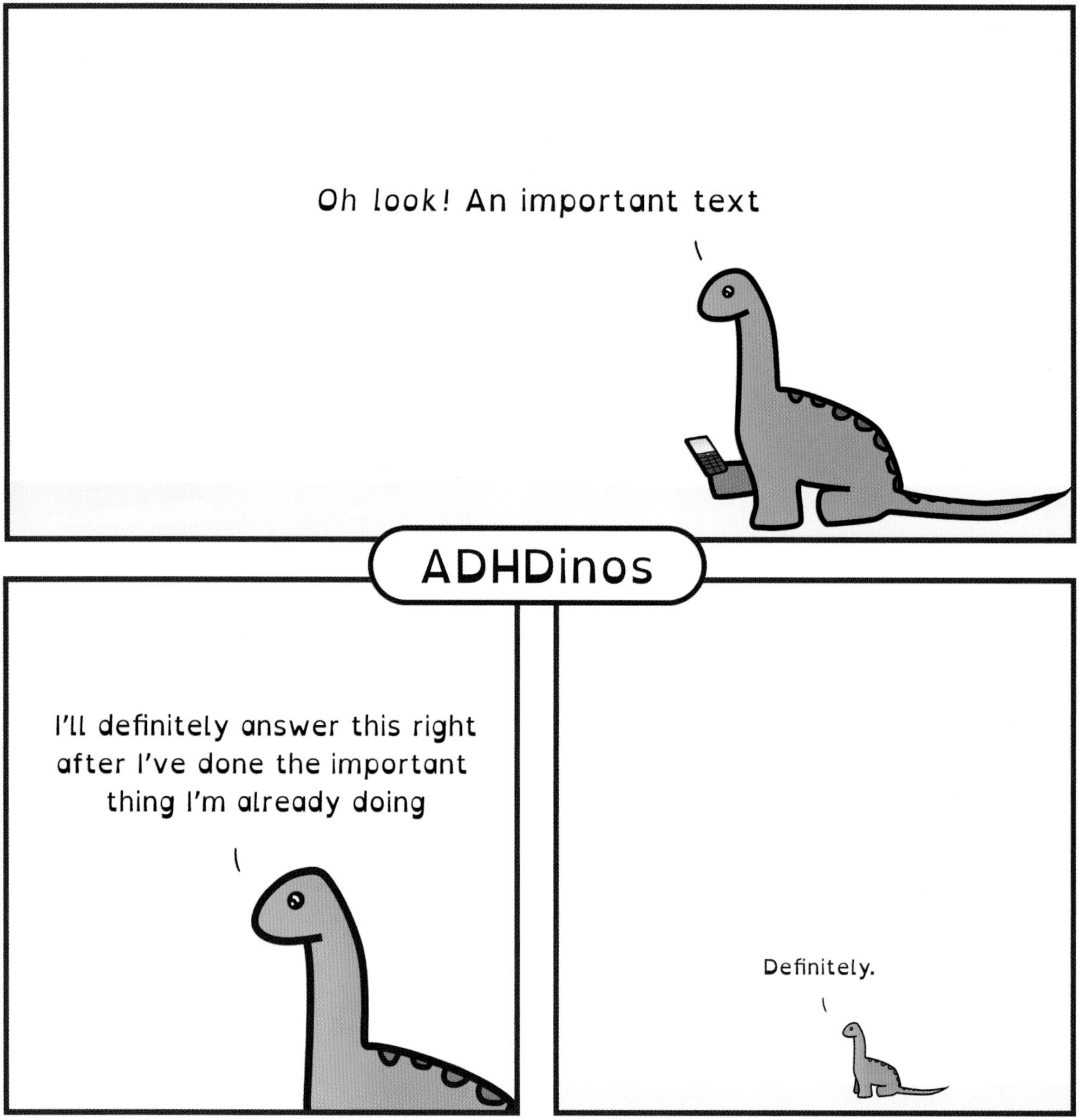
Oh look! An important text
ADHDinos
I'll definitely answer this right after I've done the important thing I'm already doing
Definitely.

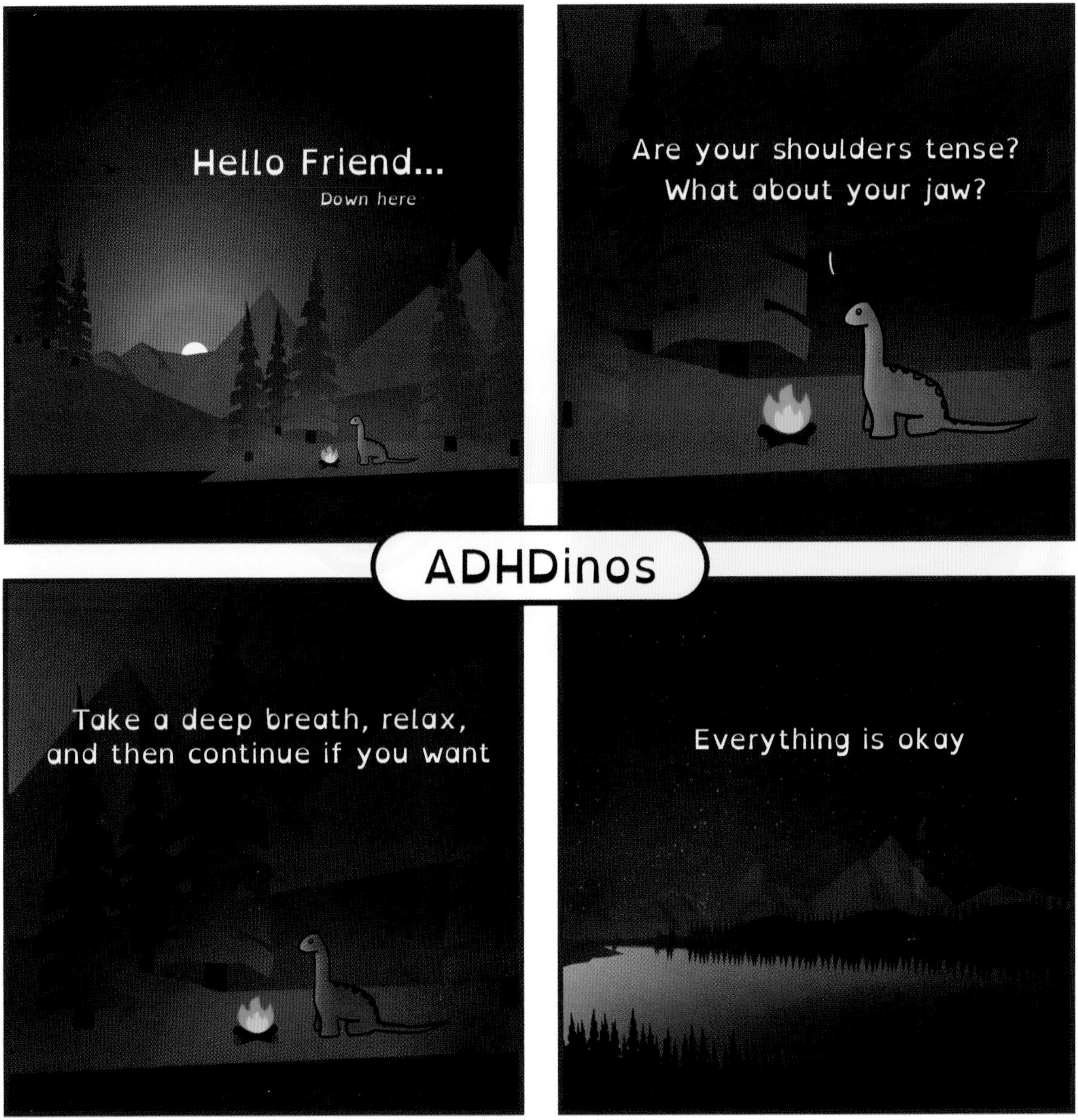
Hello Friend...
Down here
Are your shoulders tense?
What about your jaw?
ADHDinos
Take a deep breath, relax,
and then continue if you want
Everything is okay

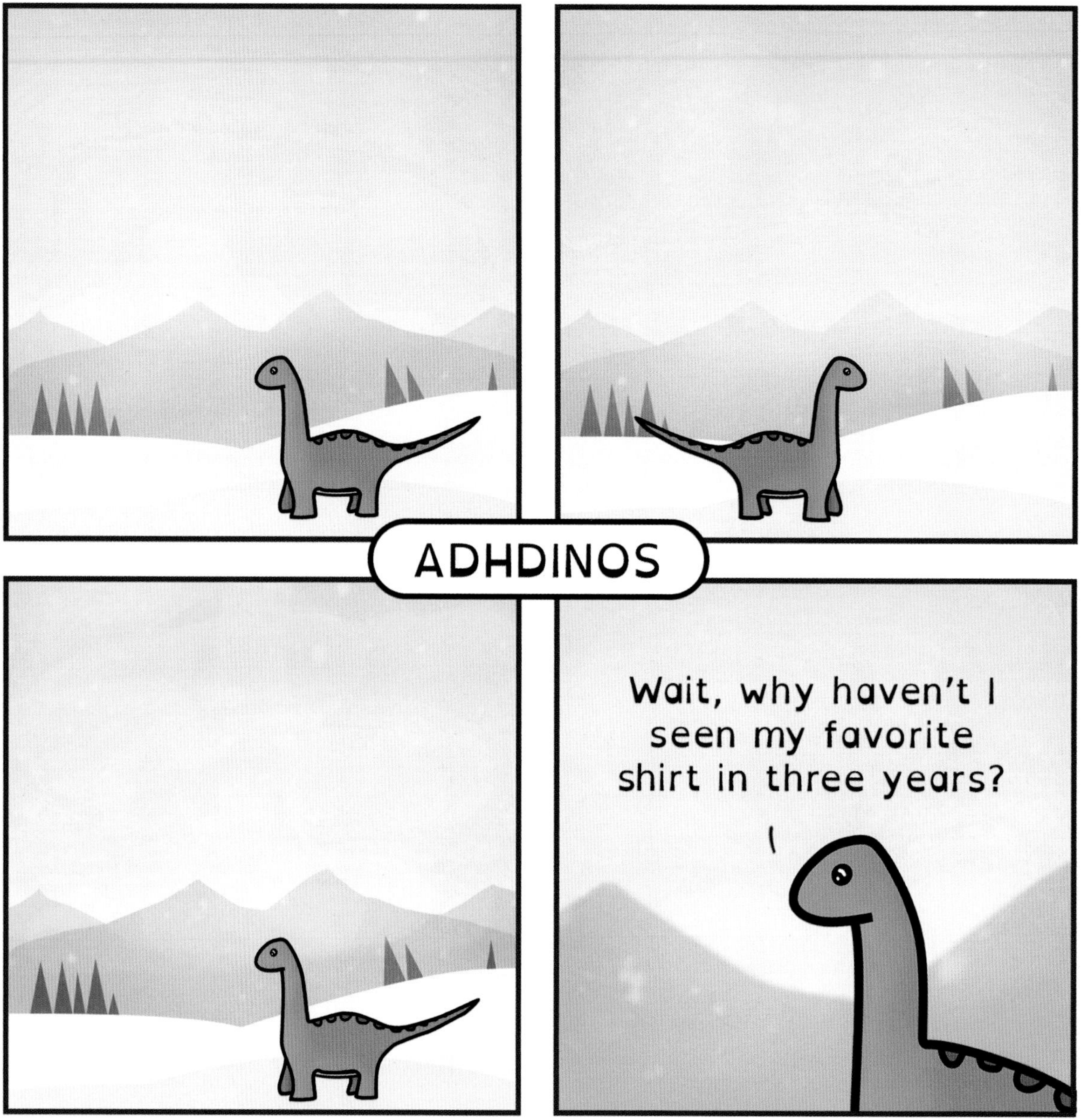
ADHDINOS
Wait, why haven't I seen my favorite shirt in three years?

Focus

When interested and engaged in a topic, individuals with ADHD do not regularly struggle with maintaining focus. When a task feels boring or repetitive, however, those with ADHD generally lose focus and motivation much more quickly than their peers.[*]

This often makes it feel impossible to pursue difficult topics and contributes greatly to impulsive or otherwise illogical decision-making, like ignoring homework despite looming consequences.

On the other hand, pursuing interesting and engaging topics Dino is passionate about has proven to be one of his greatest assets. He just has to follow these interests as they arise by engaging in them in his free time and introducing small ways to spark interest in boring or mandatory tasks.

[*] Cherry, K. What does undiagnosed ADHD look like in adults? Verywell Mind. Published April 20, 2022. https://www.verywellmind.com/what-does-undiagnosed-adhd-look-like-in-adults-5235254#

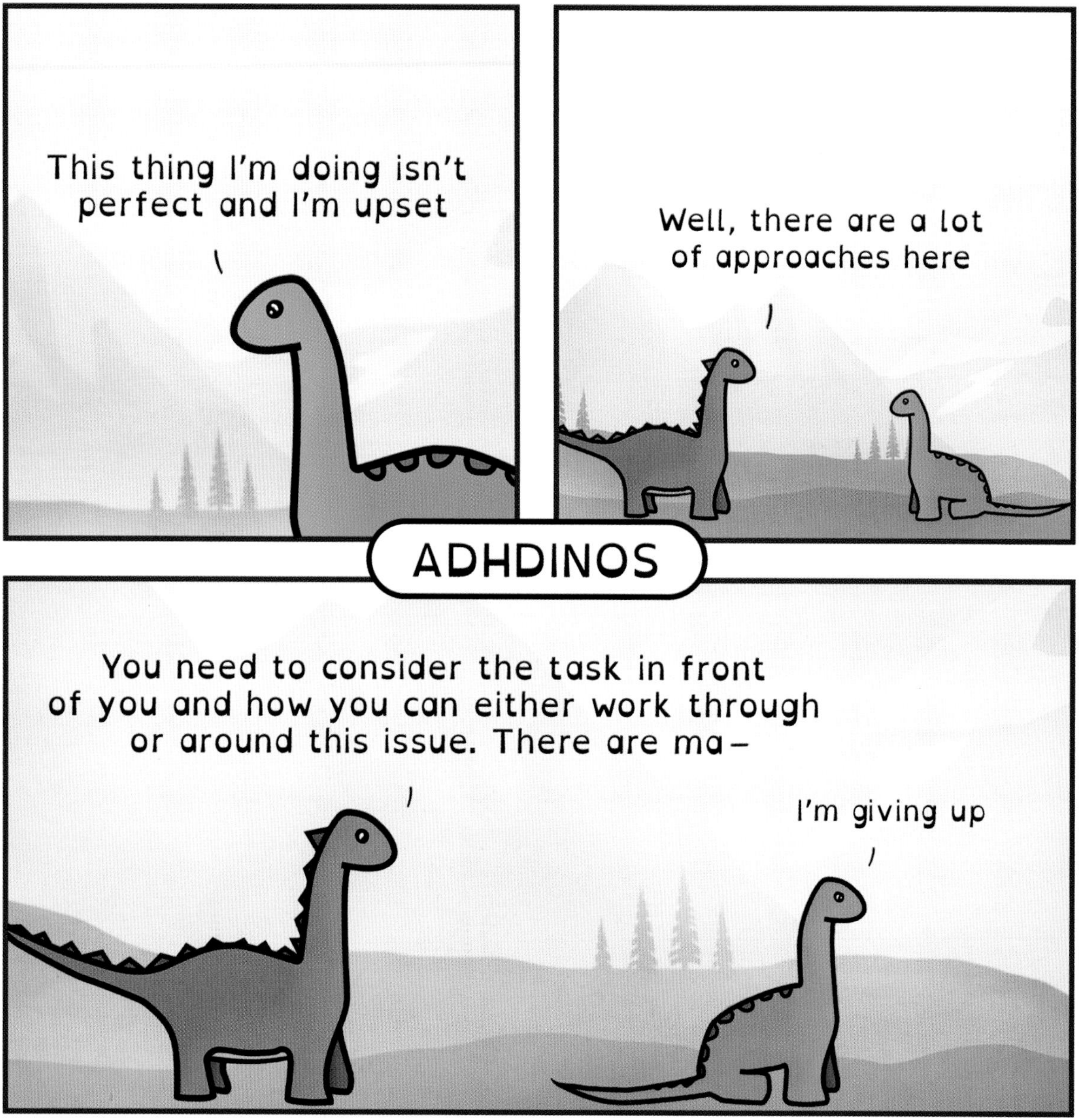
This thing I'm doing isn't perfect and I'm upset
Well, there are a lot of approaches here
ADHDINOS
You need to consider the task in front of you and how you can either work through or around this issue. There are ma–
I'm giving up

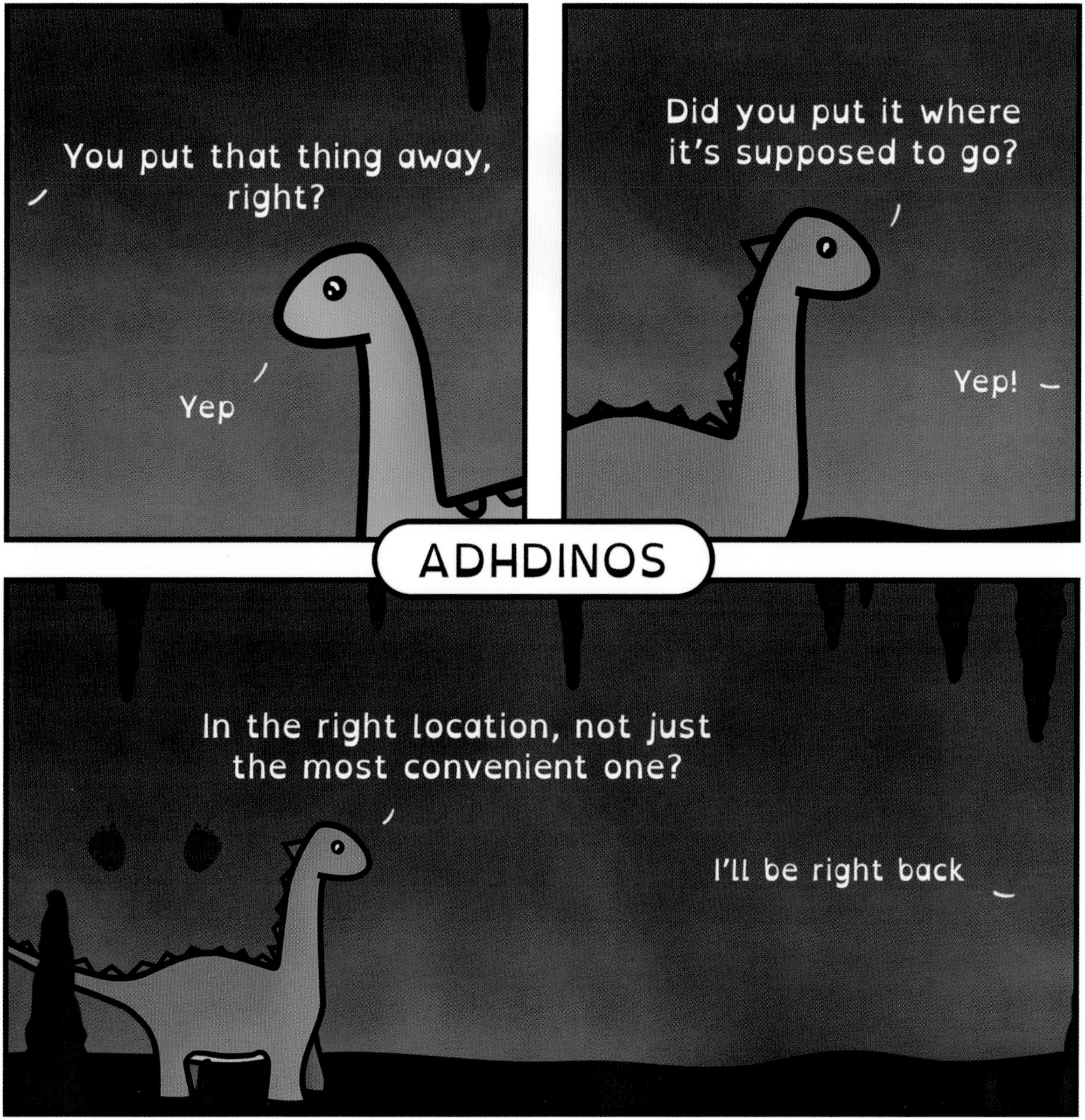
You put that thing away, right?
Yep
Did you put it where it's supposed to go?
Yep!
ADHDINOS
In the right location, not just the most convenient one?
I'll be right back

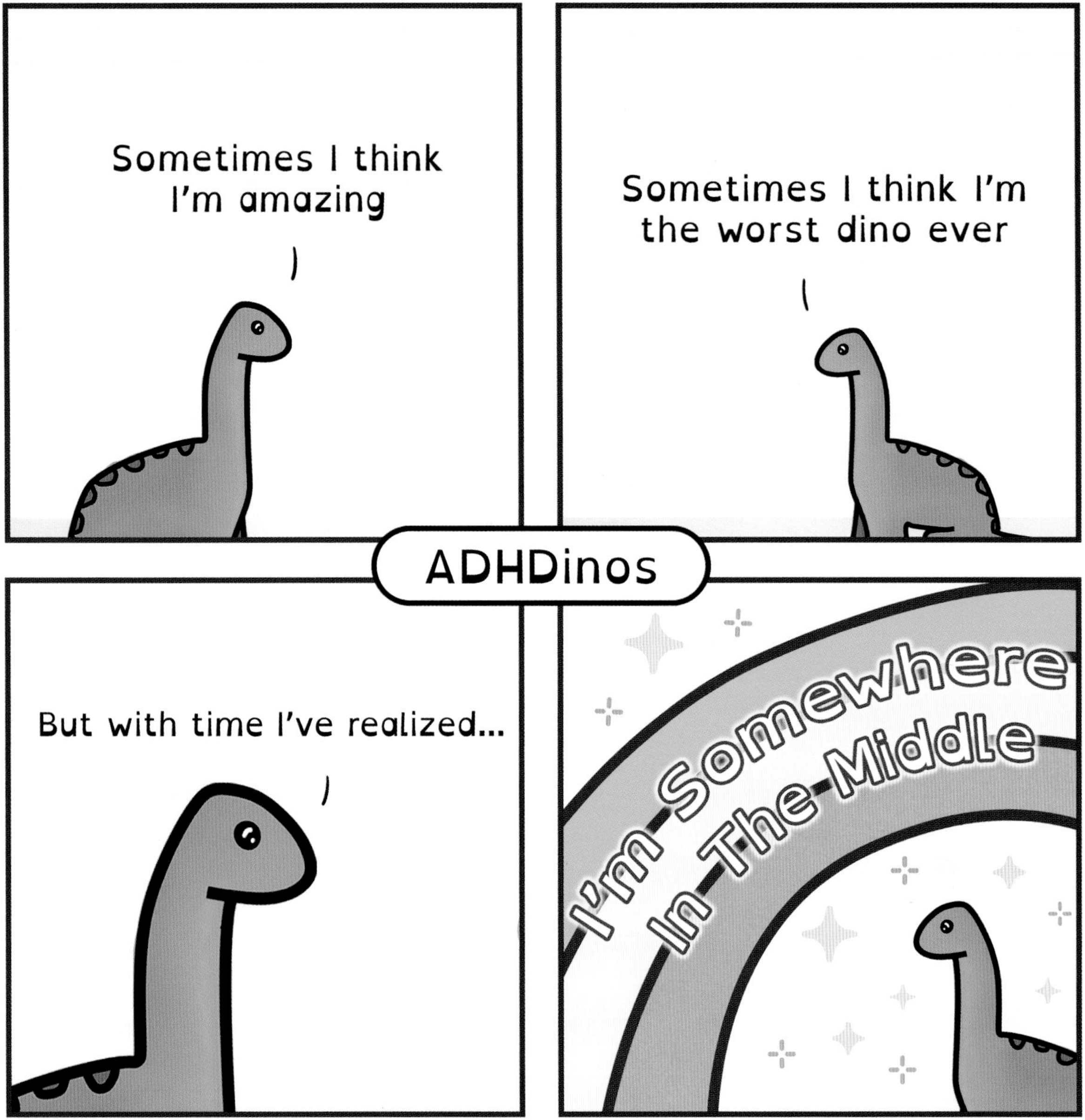
Sometimes I think I'm amazing
Sometimes I think I'm the worst dino ever
ADHDinos
But with time I've realized...
I'm Somewhere In The Middle

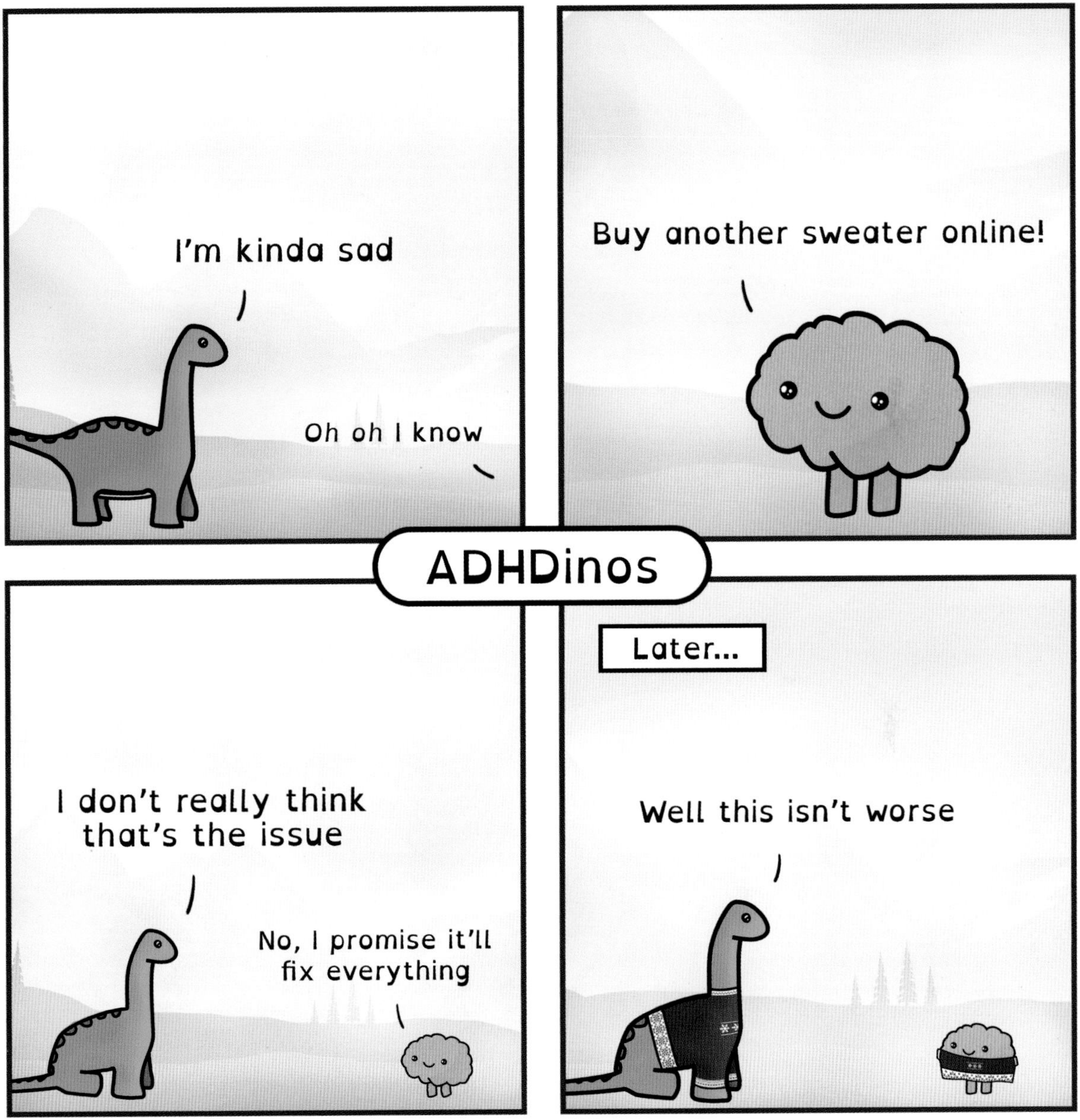
I'm kinda sad
Oh oh I know
Buy another sweater online!
ADHDinos
I don't really think that's the issue
No, I promise it'll fix everything
Later...
Well this isn't worse

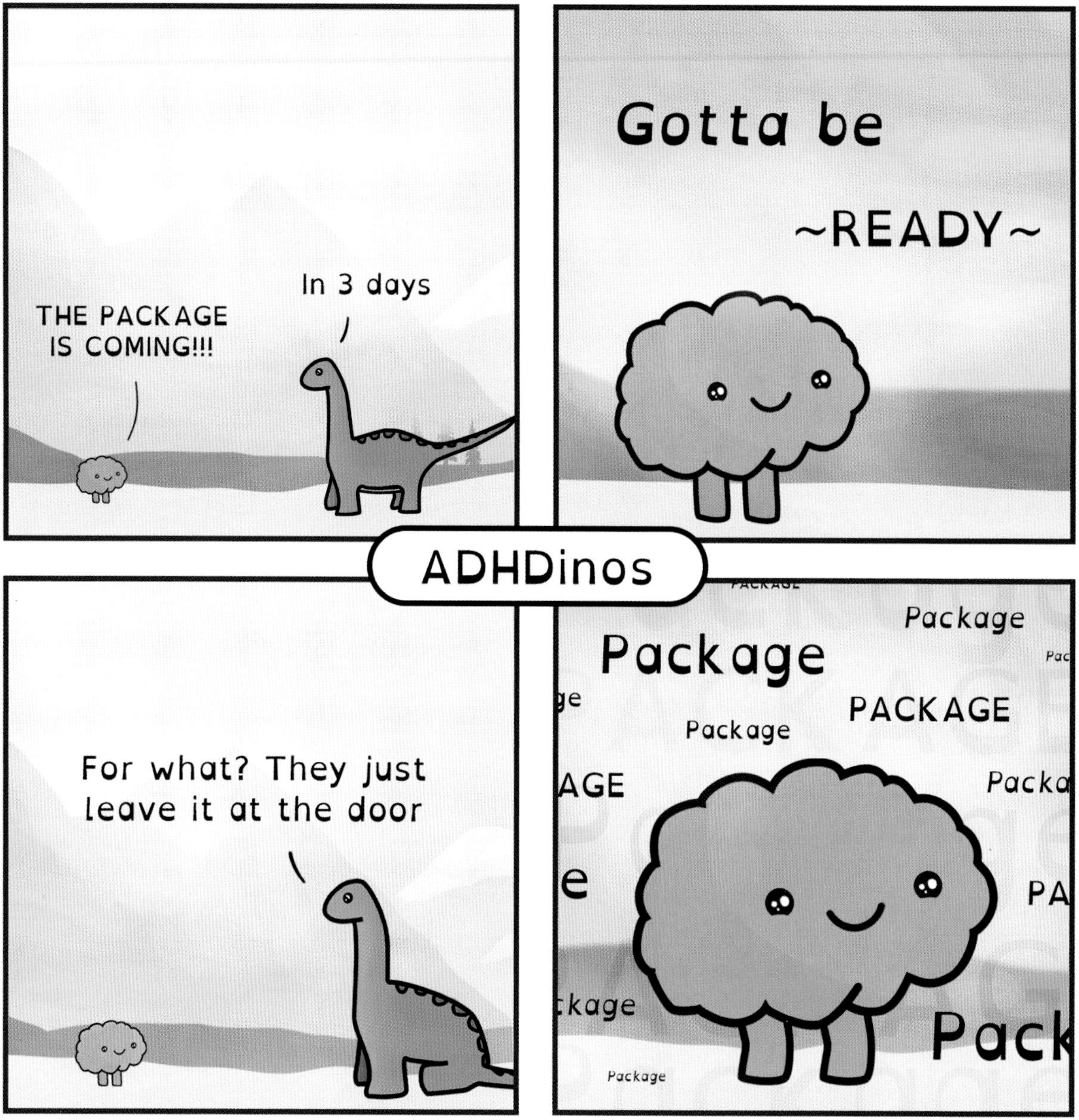
THE PACKAGE IS COMING!!!
In 3 days
Gotta be
~READY~
ADHDinos
For what? They just leave it at the door
Package
Package
PACKAGE
Package
Package

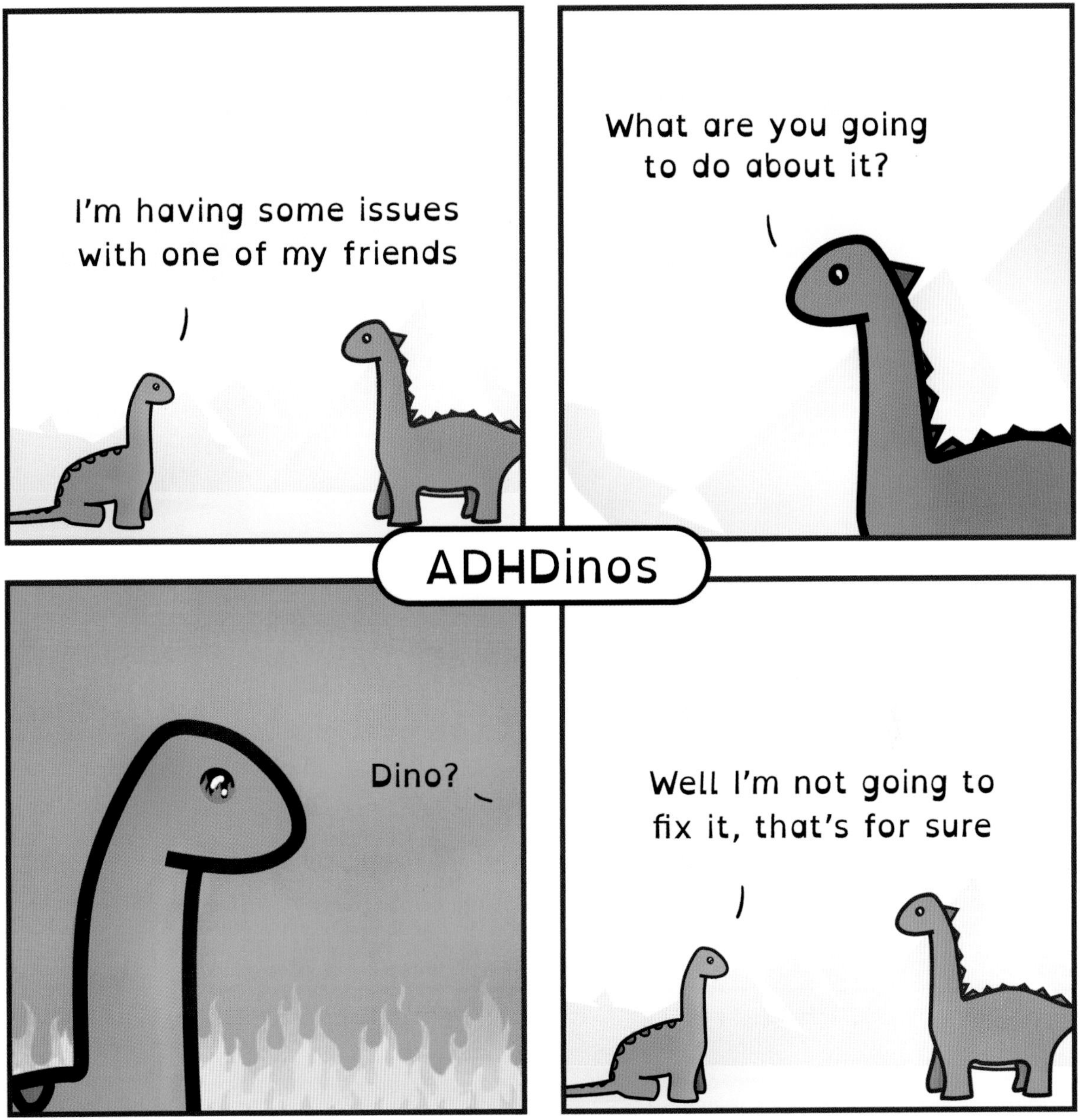
I'm having some issues
with one of my friends
What are you going
to do about it?
ADHDinos
Dino?
Well I'm not going to
fix it, that's for sure

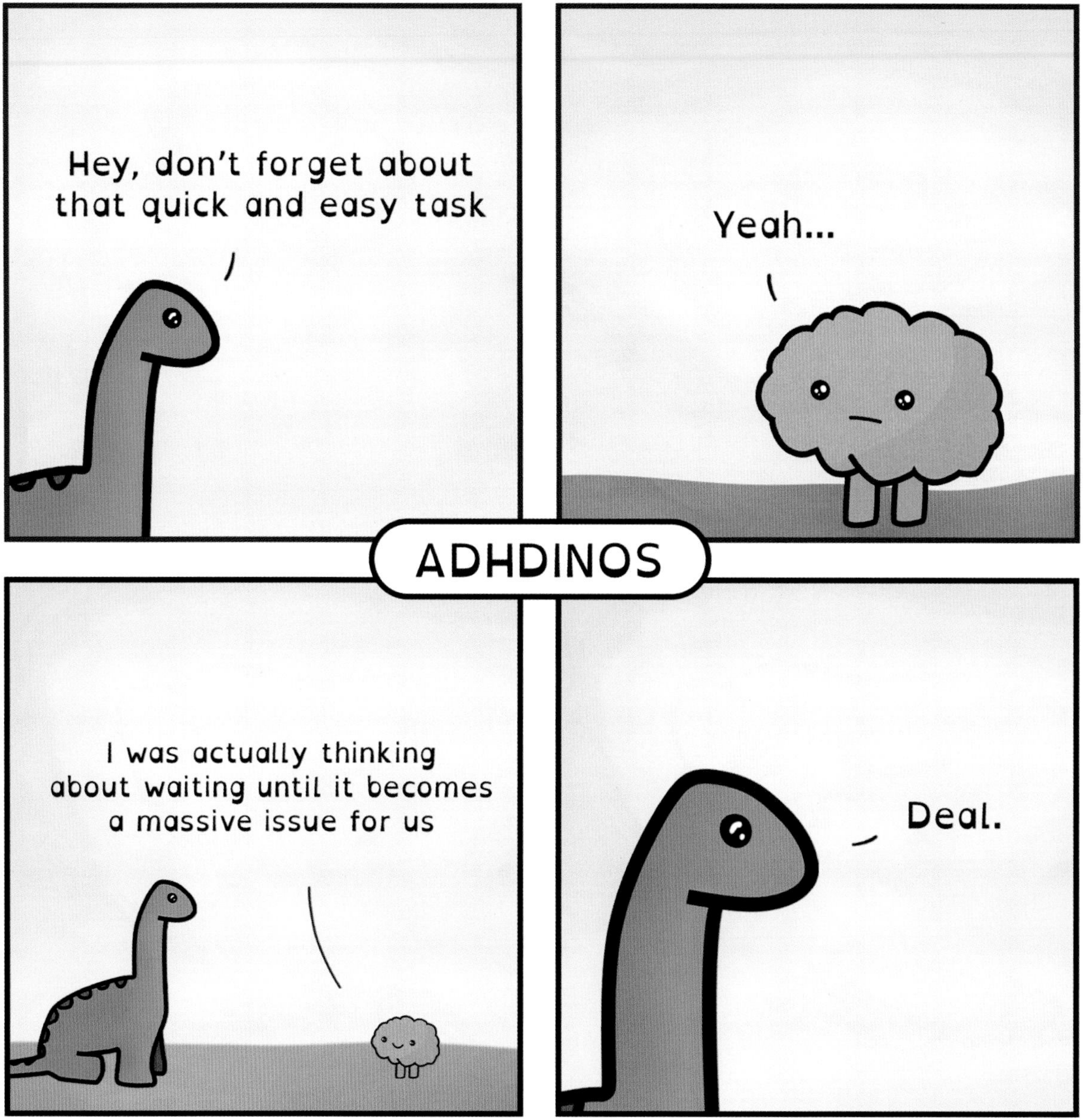
Hey, don't forget about that quick and easy task
Yeah...
ADHDINOS
I was actually thinking about waiting until it becomes a massive issue for us
Deal.

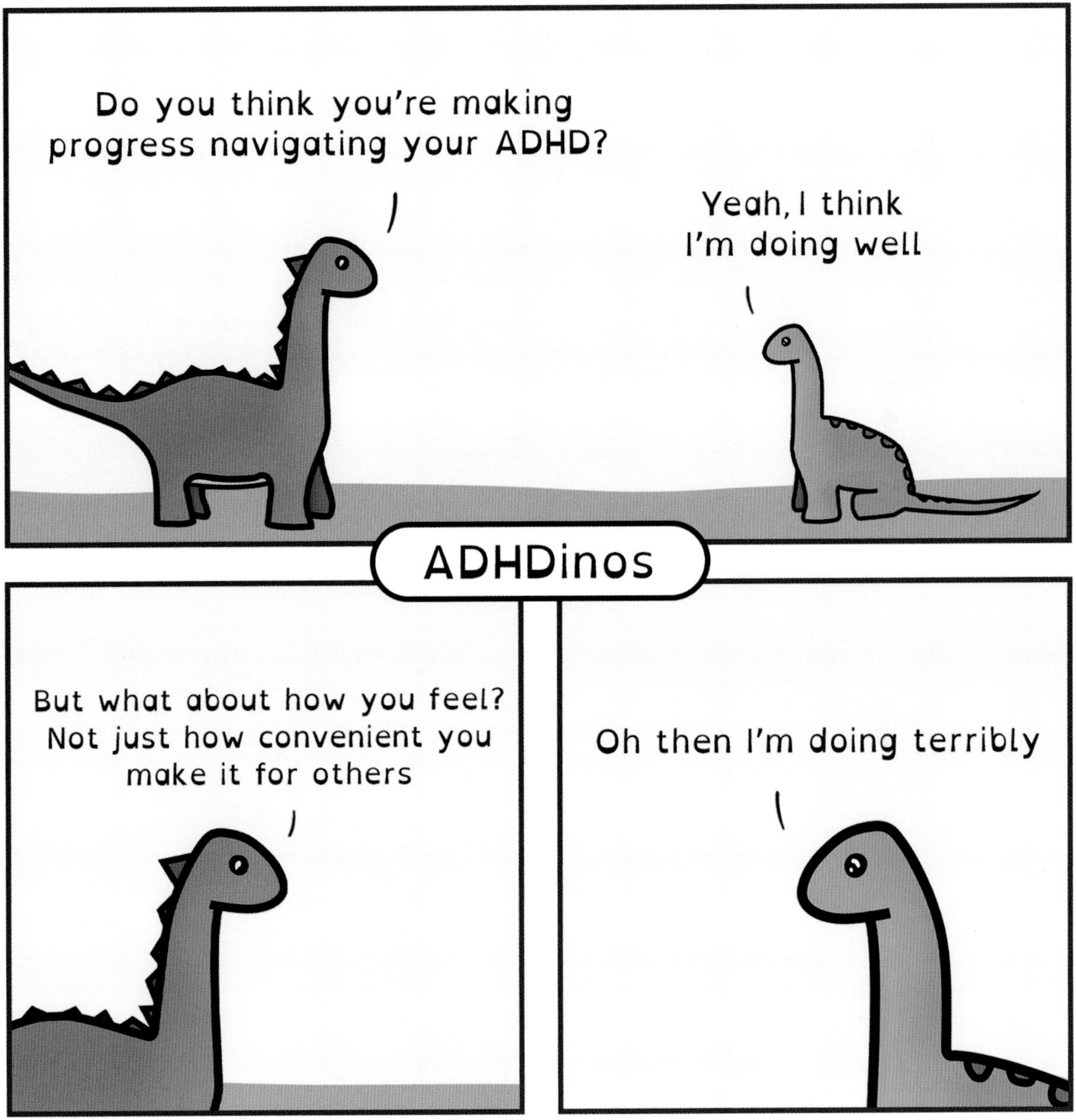
Do you think you're making progress navigating your ADHD?
Yeah, I think I'm doing well
ADHDinos
But what about how you feel? Not just how convenient you make it for others
Oh then I'm doing terribly

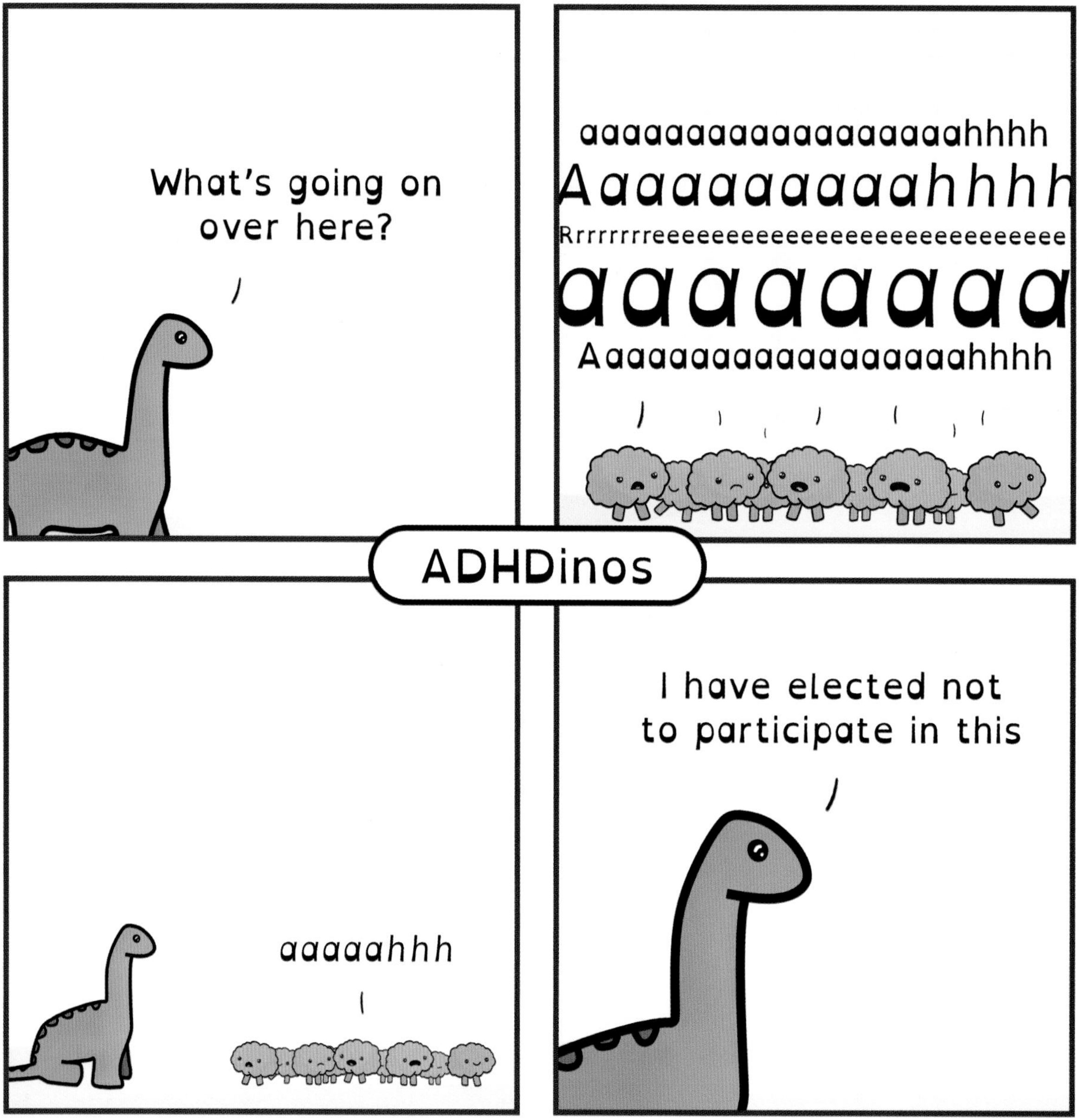
What's going on over here?
aaaaaaaaaaaaaaaaaaahhhh
Aaaaaaaaaaaahhhh
Rrrrrrrreeeeeeeeeeeeeeeeeeeeeeeeeeee
aaaaaaaaa
Aaaaaaaaaaaaaaaaaaahhhh
ADHDinos
aaaaahhh
I have elected not to participate in this

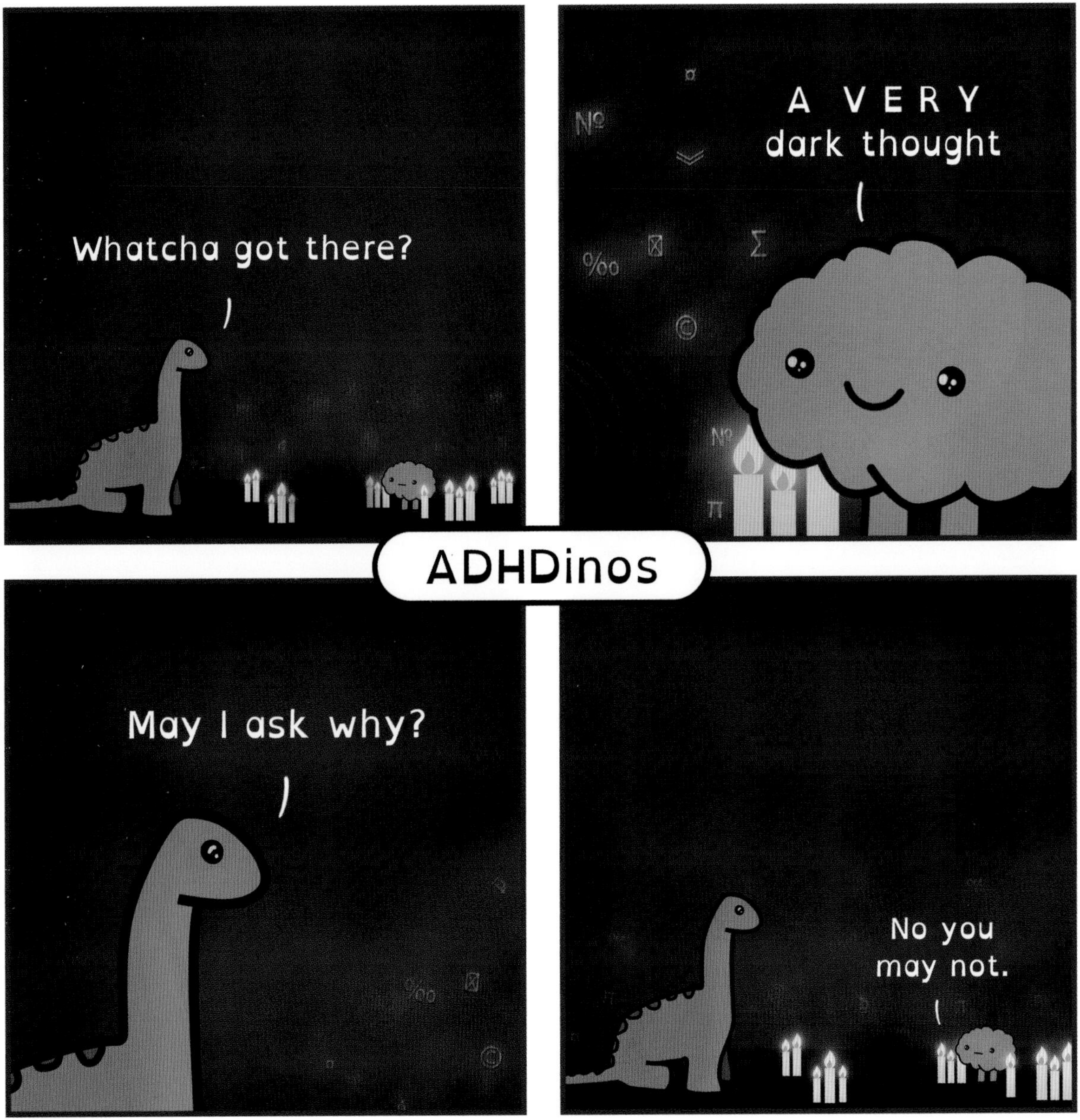

Whatcha got there?
A VERY dark thought
ADHDinos
May I ask why?
No you may not.

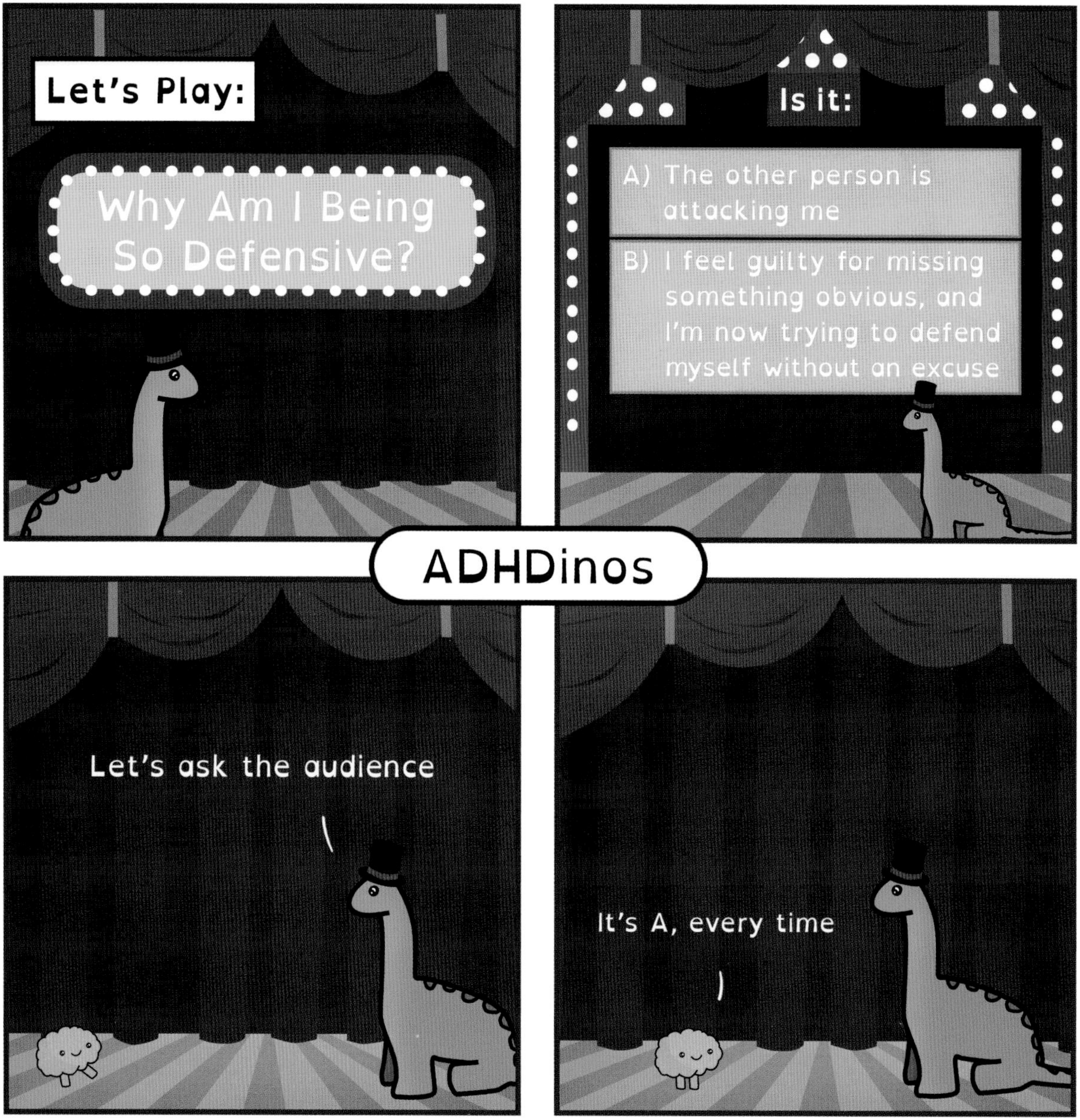
Let's Play:
Why Am I Being So Defensive?
Is it:
A) The other person is attacking me
B) I feel guilty for missing something obvious, and I'm now trying to defend myself without an excuse
ADHDinos
Let's ask the audience
It's A, every time

"Blame"

Dino forgets many things, and this can really impact him negatively. He often won't know what to do in response to a problem because he can't recall what caused the problem in the first place, which also means he can't offer a valid excuse. He frequently forgets small things, like calling someone when he needs to, booking an important appointment, handing in a form, or putting something away. Each of these seems minor on its own but can result in big consequences.

Dino fears that if he accepts all of the blame when these sorts of things happen, it will make him look careless or bad. He really wishes he could rationalize these mistakes, but he rarely can. This puts him in a lot of situations where he overcompensates for his lack of an excuse with defensiveness.

Dino has been learning to take a step back when this may be happening. By looking at where he actually went wrong instead of trying to reassign blame, he can work to prevent a similar mistake in the future.

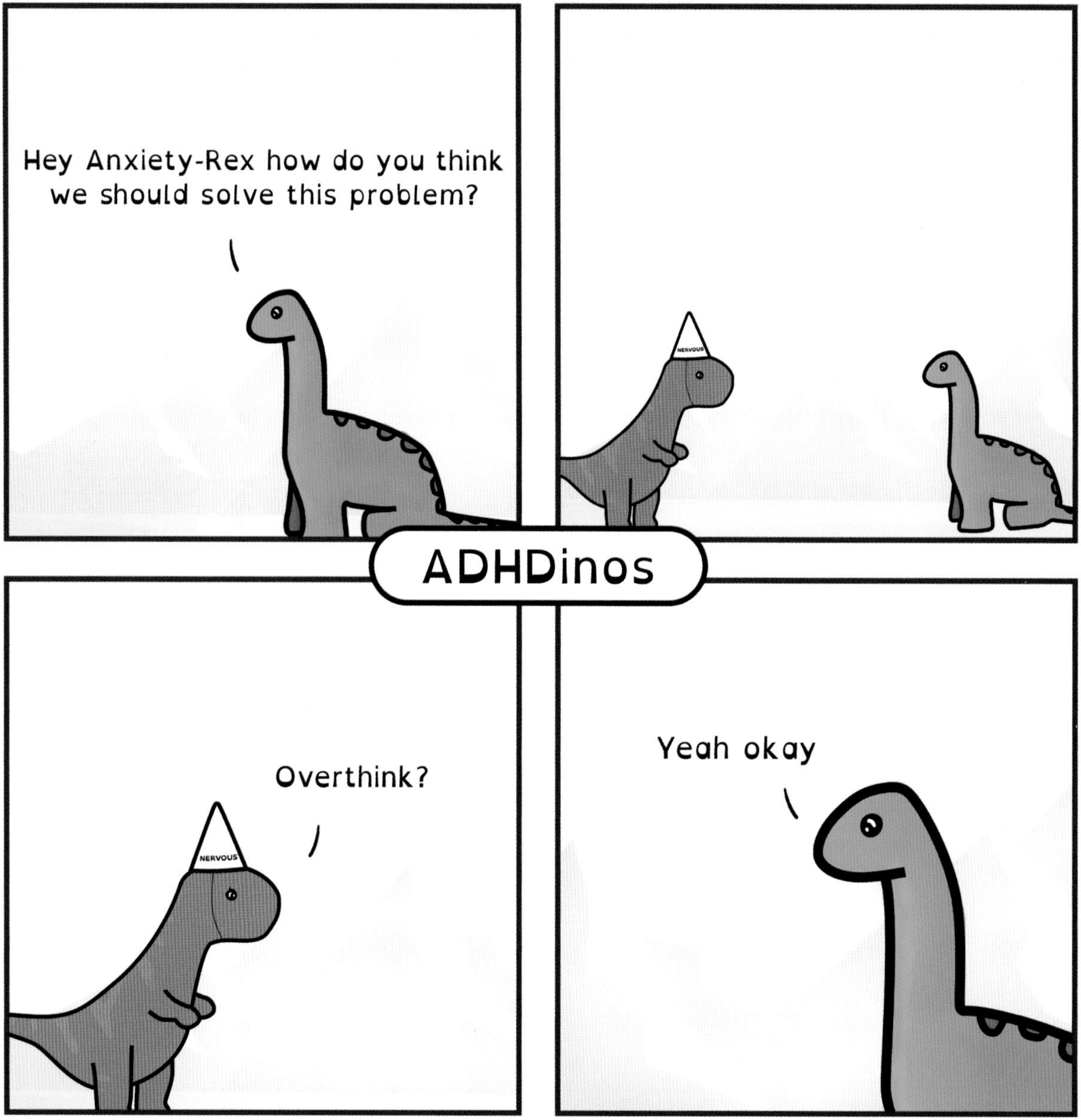

Hey Anxiety-Rex how do you think we should solve this problem?
NERVOUS
ADHDinos
NERVOUS
Overthink?
Yeah okay

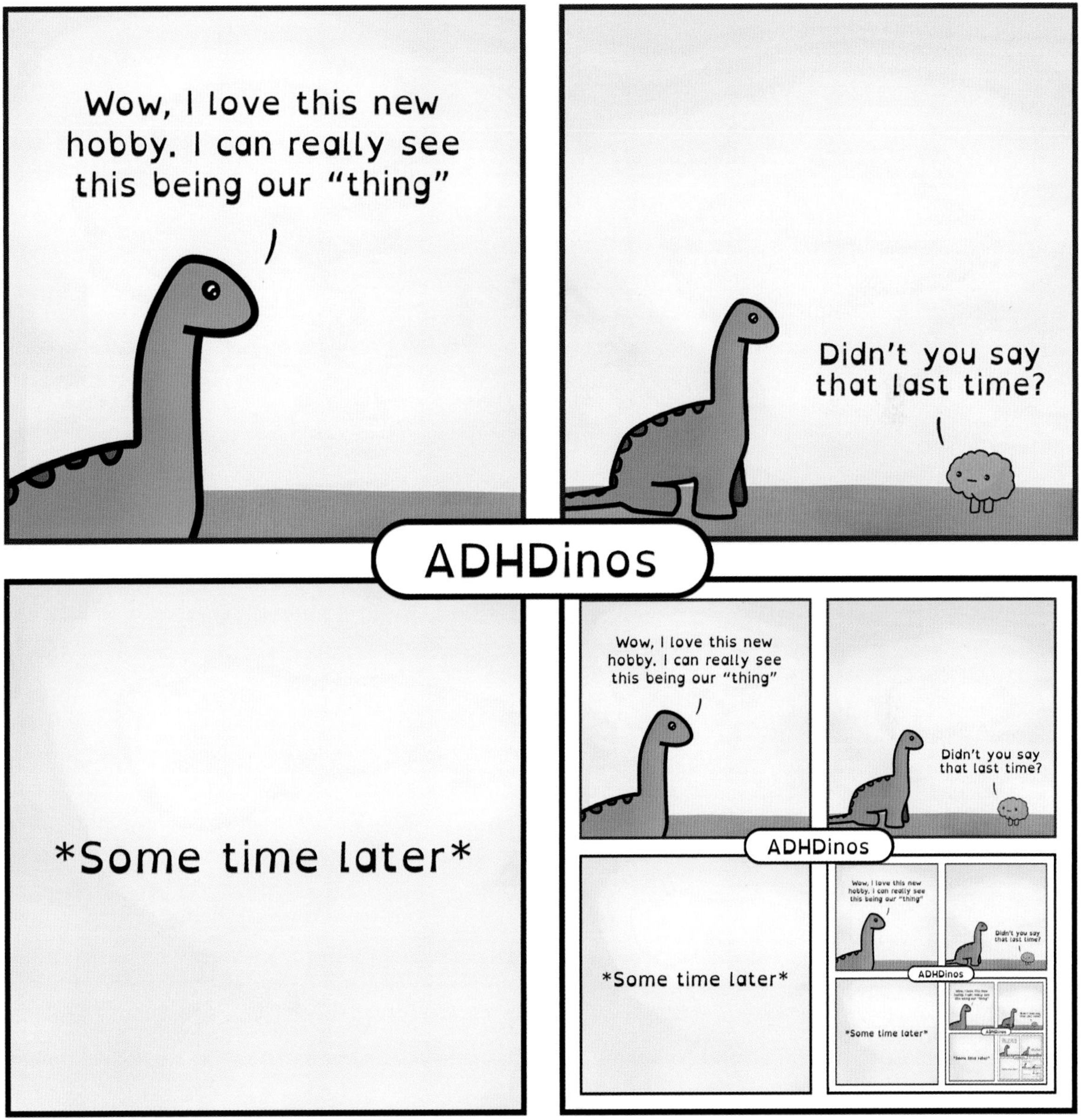

Wow, I love this new hobby. I can really see this being our "thing"
Didn't you say that last time?
ADHDinos
Some time later
Wow, I love this new hobby. I can really see this being our "thing"
Didn't you say that last time?
ADHDinos
Some time later

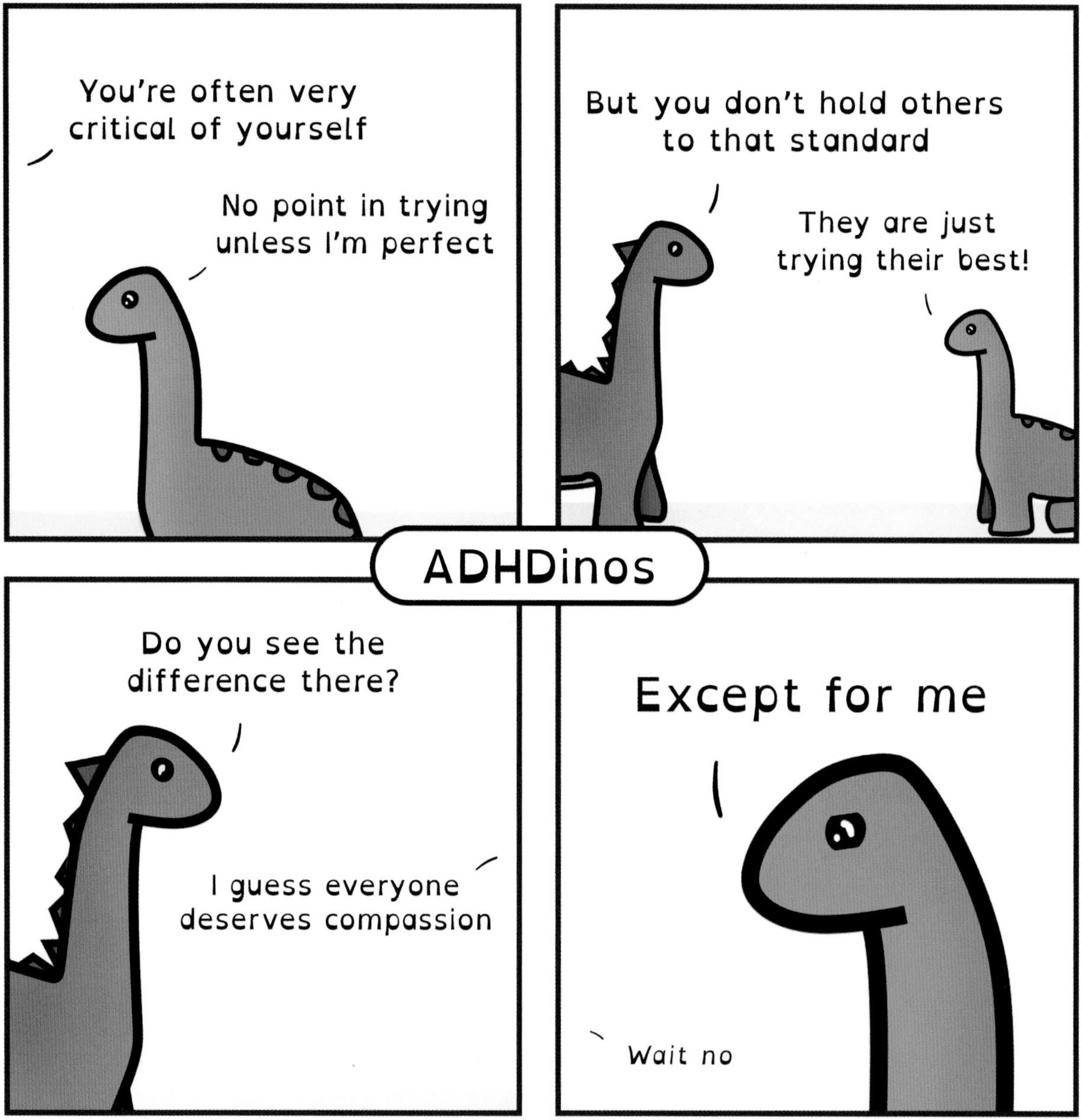
You're often very critical of yourself
No point in trying unless I'm perfect
But you don't hold others to that standard
They are just trying their best!
ADHDinos
Do you see the difference there?
I guess everyone deserves compassion
Except for me
Wait no

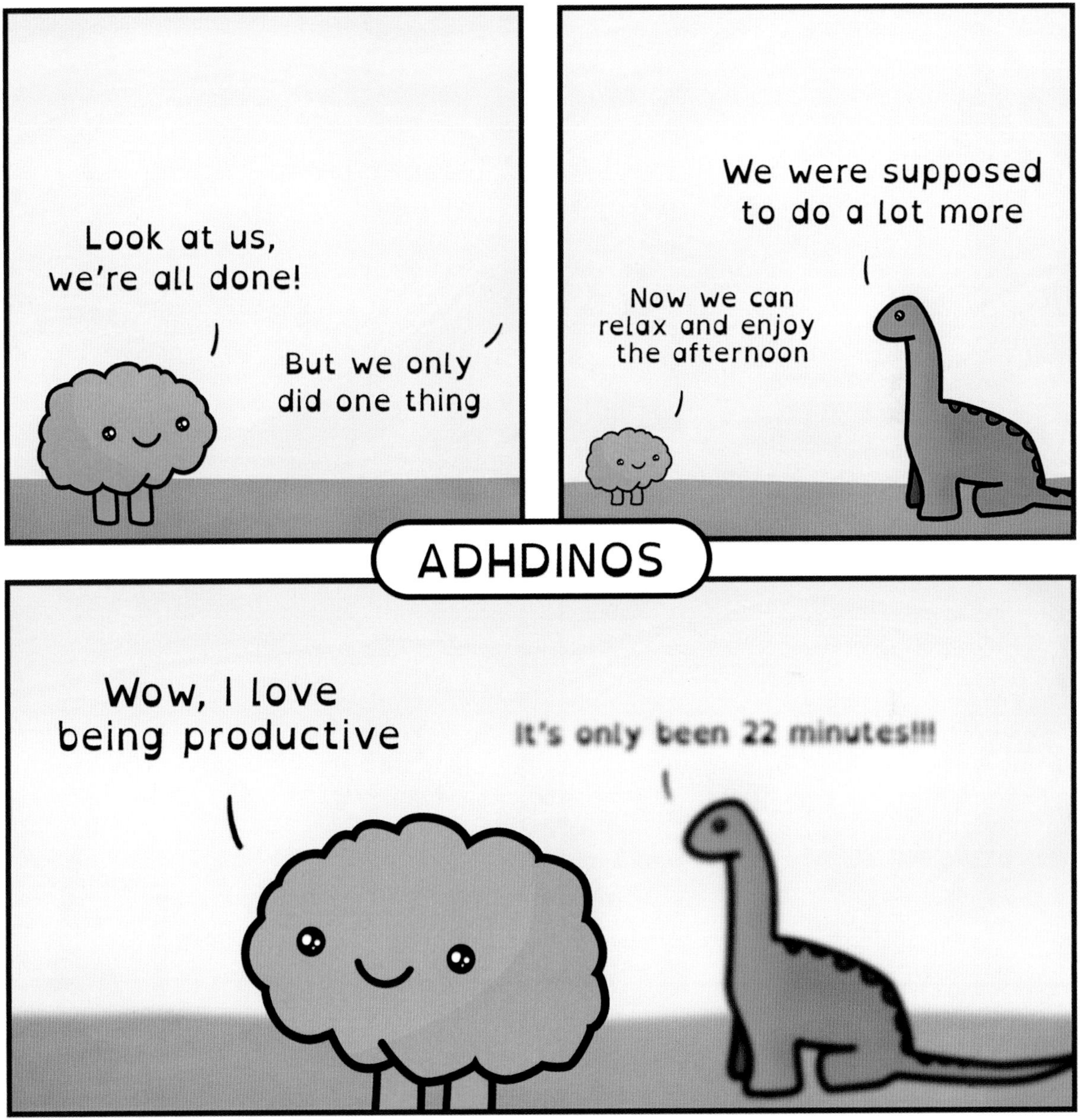
Look at us, we're all done!
But we only did one thing
We were supposed to do a lot more
Now we can relax and enjoy the afternoon
ADHDINOS
Wow, I love being productive
It's only been 22 minutes!!!

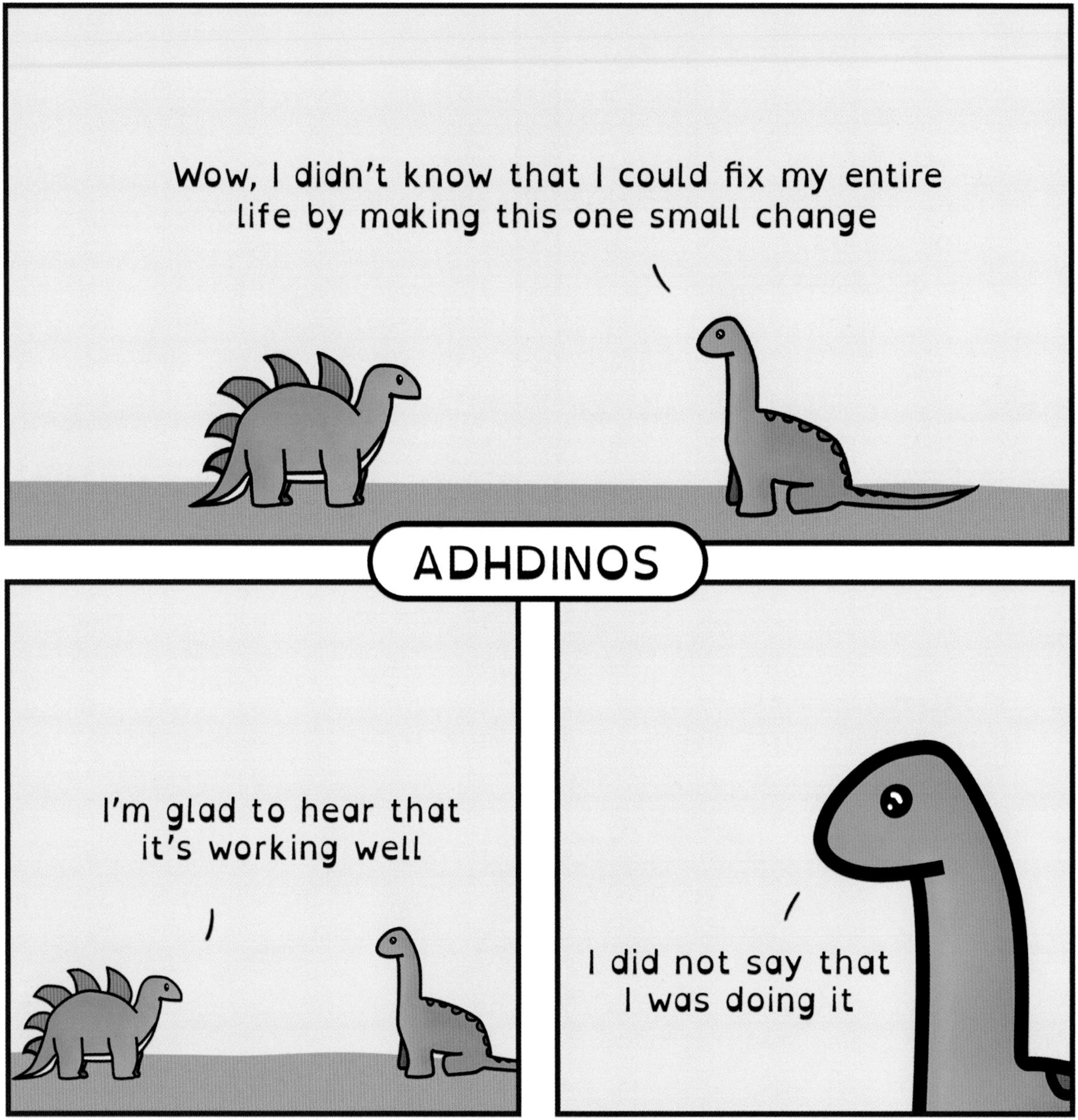
Wow, I didn't know that I could fix my entire life by making this one small change
ADHDINOS
I'm glad to hear that it's working well
I did not say that I was doing it

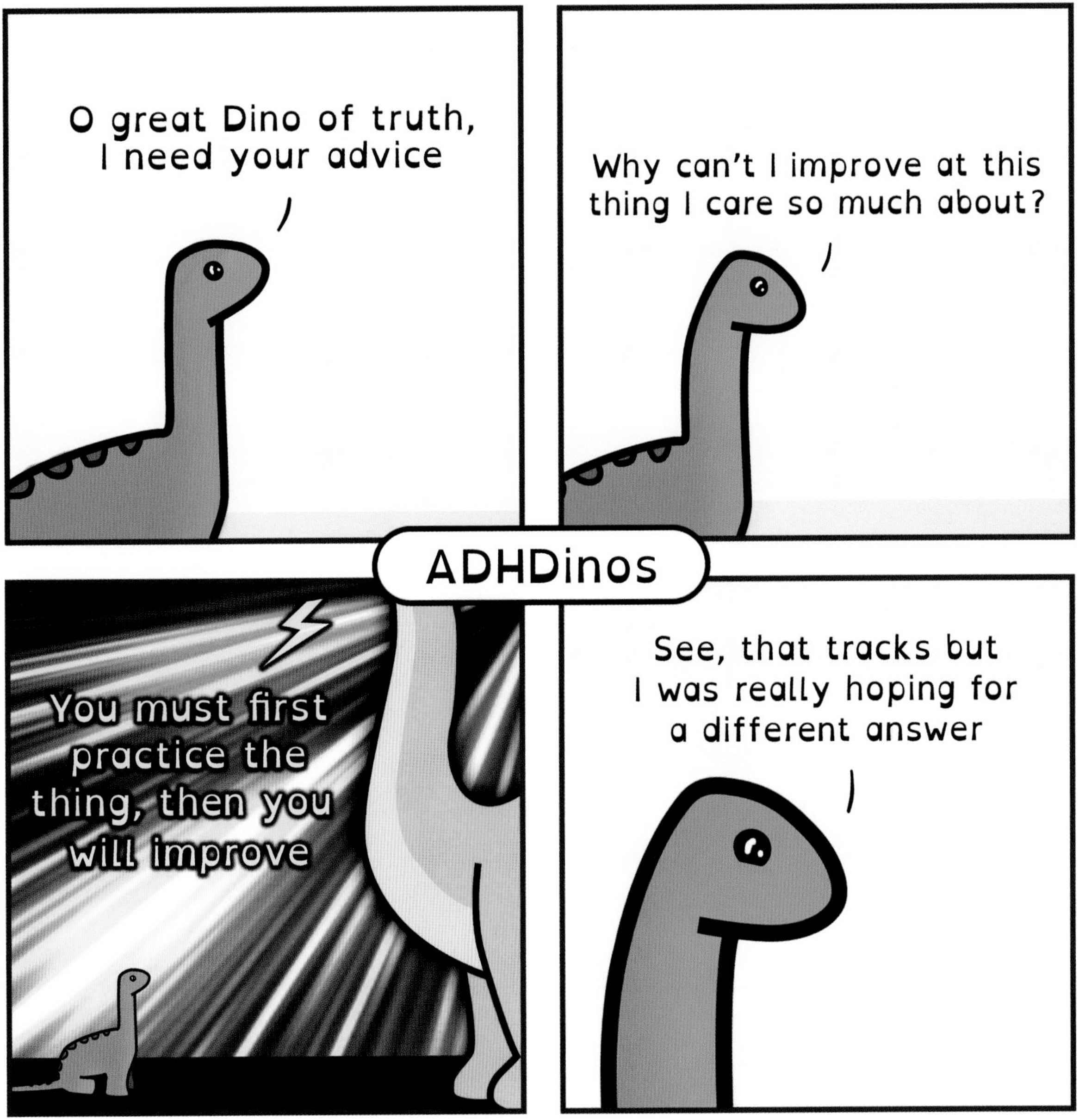
O great Dino of truth, I need your advice
Why can't I improve at this thing I care so much about?
ADHDinos
You must first practice the thing, then you will improve
See, that tracks but I was really hoping for a different answer

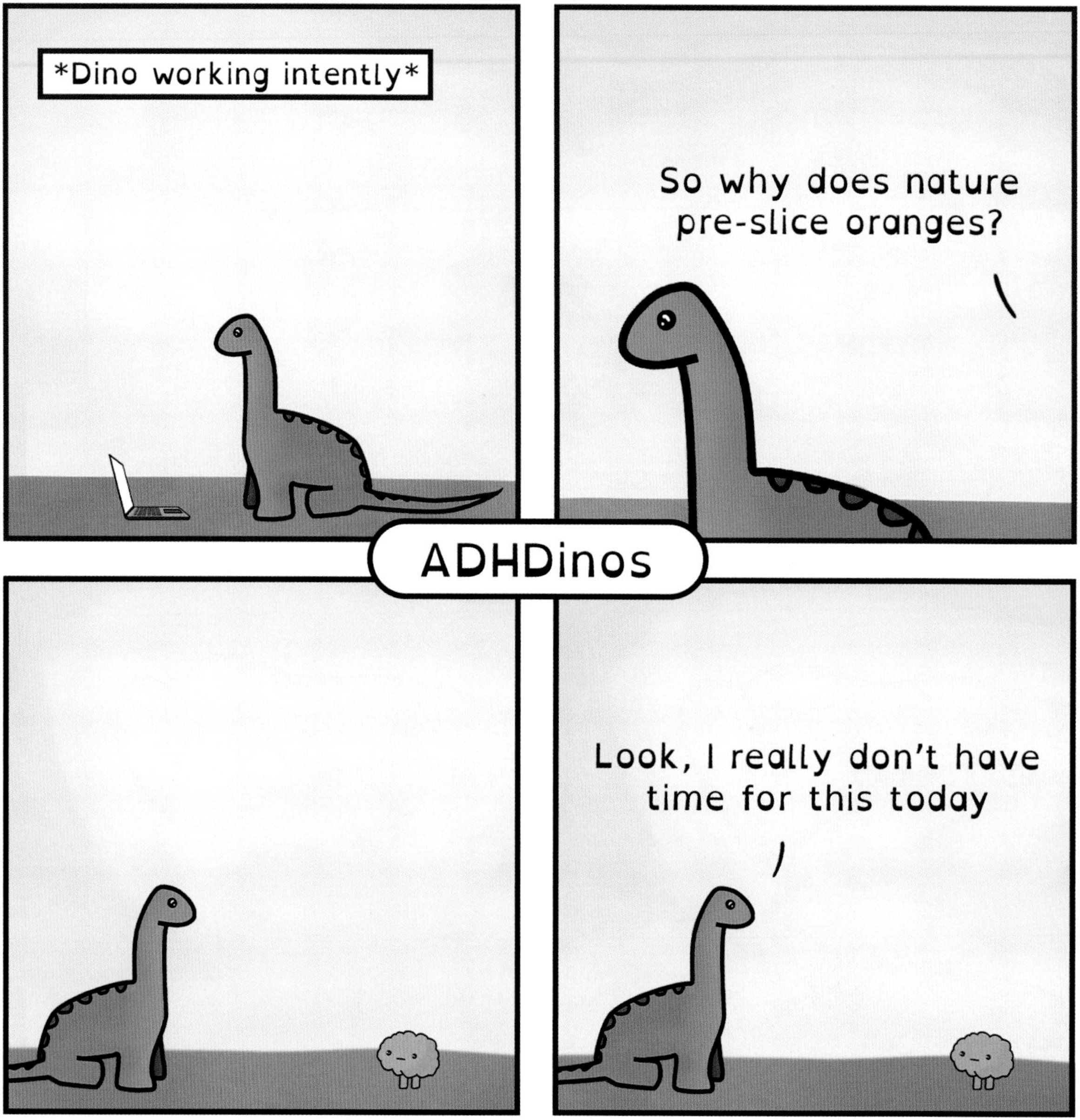
Dino working intently
So why does nature pre-slice oranges?
ADHDinos
Look, I really don't have time for this today

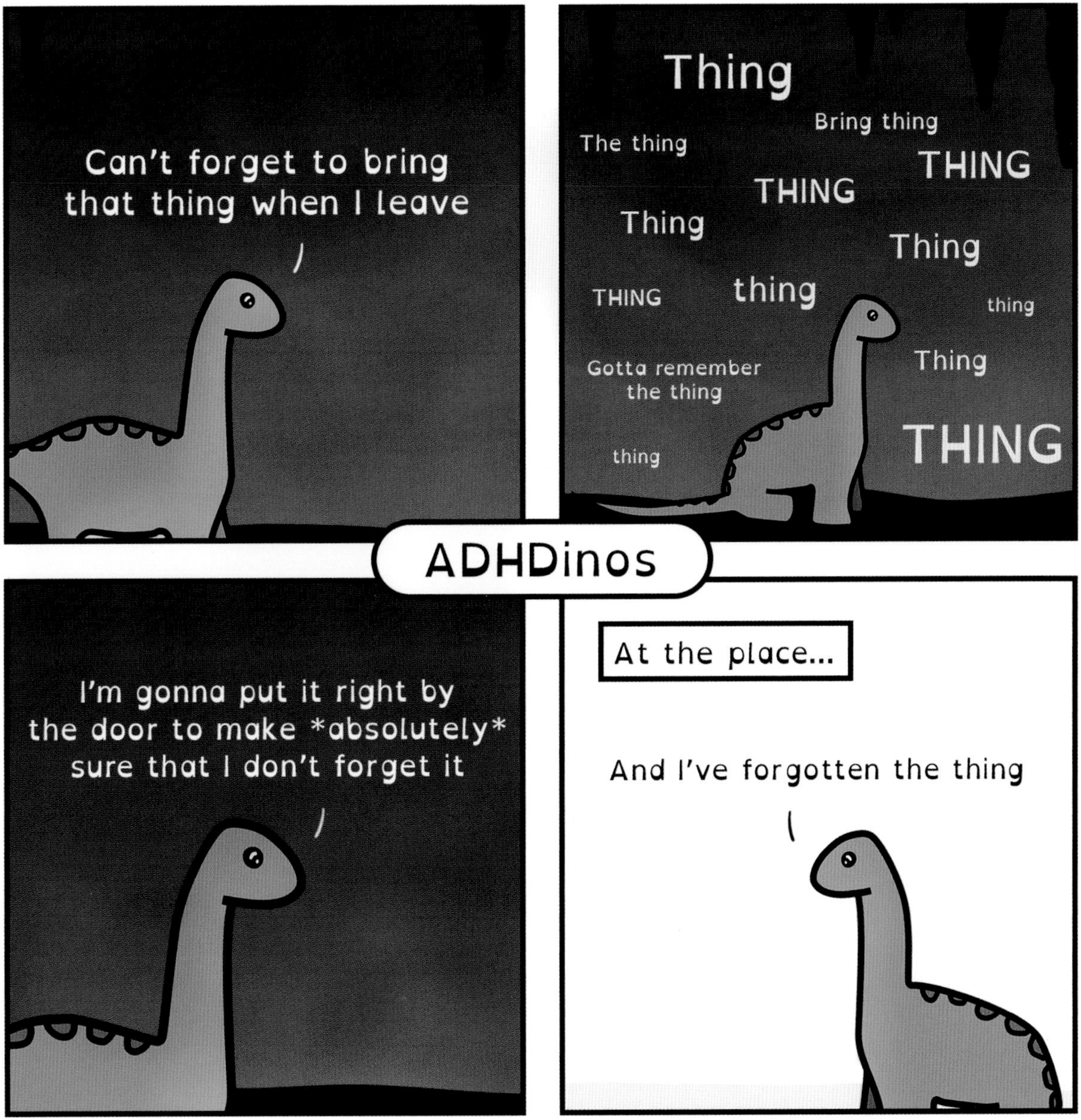
Can't forget to bring that thing when I leave
Thing
Bring thing
The thing
THING
THING
Thing
Thing
THING
thing
thing
Gotta remember the thing
Thing
THING
thing
ADHDinos
I'm gonna put it right by the door to make *absolutely* sure that I don't forget it
At the place...
And I've forgotten the thing

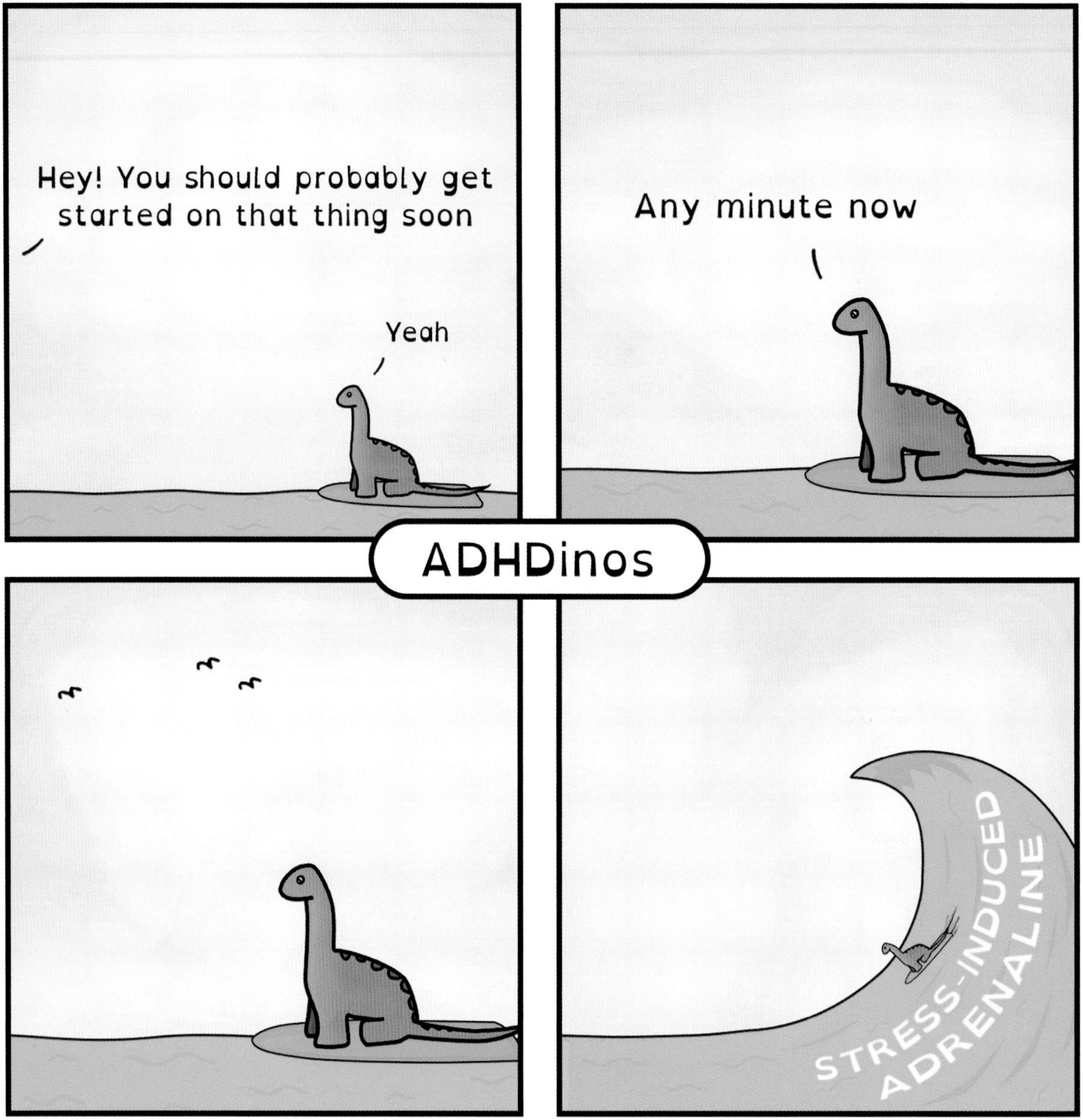
Hey! You should probably get started on that thing soon
Yeah
Any minute now
ADHDinos
STRESS-INDUCED ADRENALINE

Motivation

Fundamentally, motivation is the willpower to take on a task. Individuals with ADHD struggle with executive function—the ability to plan and execute tasks.

When it comes to initiating tasks, looming consequences do not motivate Dino to spring into action. If something can be put off until a later date, it likely will be. After leaving a task until the last minute, hyperfocus will take over out of necessity, and Dino will usually complete the task remarkably fast, though not always as well as he might have done otherwise.

What's specifically problematic about this tendency is how stress and adrenaline-induced hyperfocus can shift from a helpful ability Dino can call upon in a pinch to a problematic and unhealthy crutch he relies on to get almost all of his major projects done. This is fundamentally unsustainable and is a major contributor to other issues, such as stress and burnout.

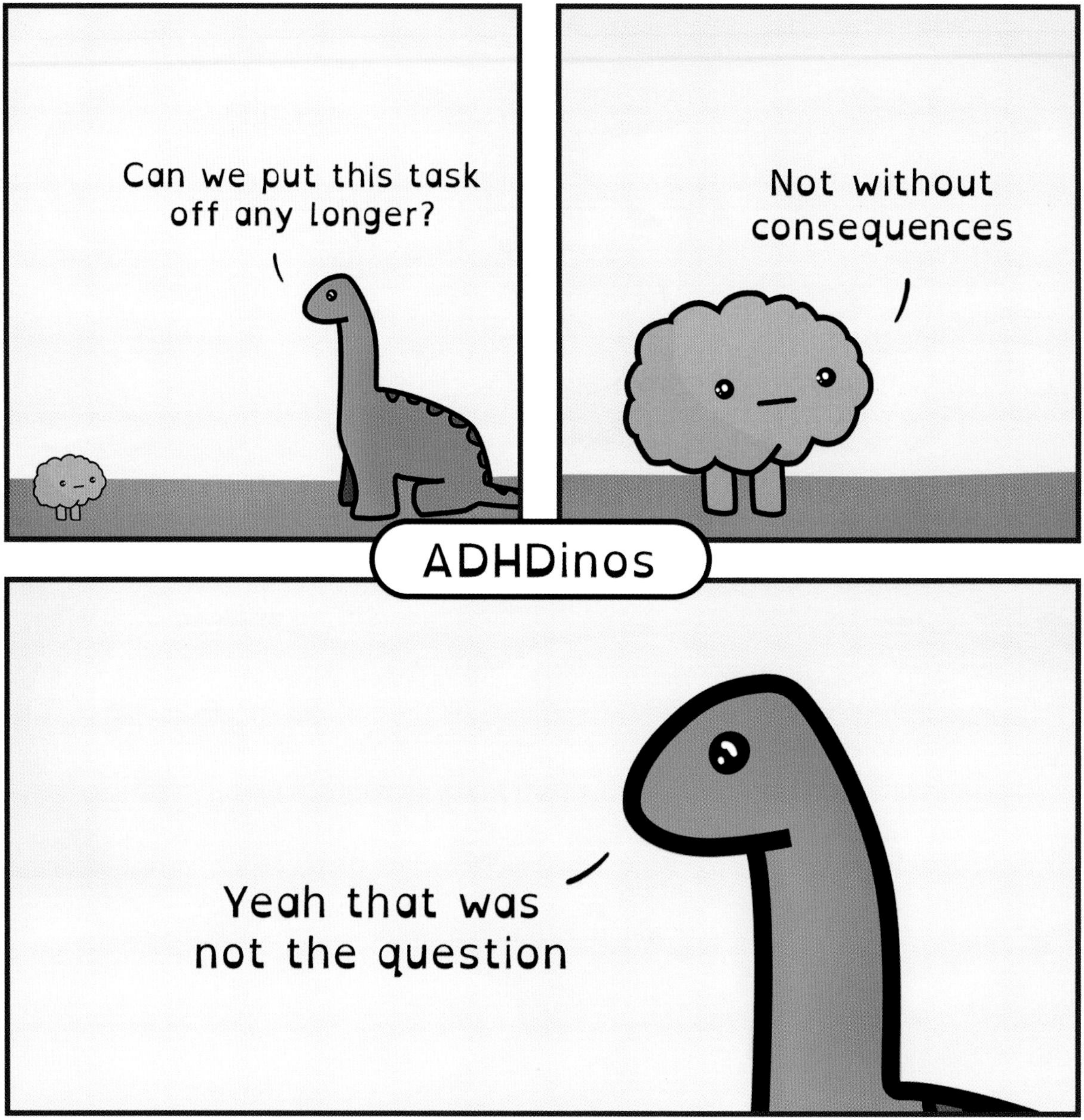
Can we put this task off any longer?
Not without consequences
ADHDinos
Yeah that was not the question

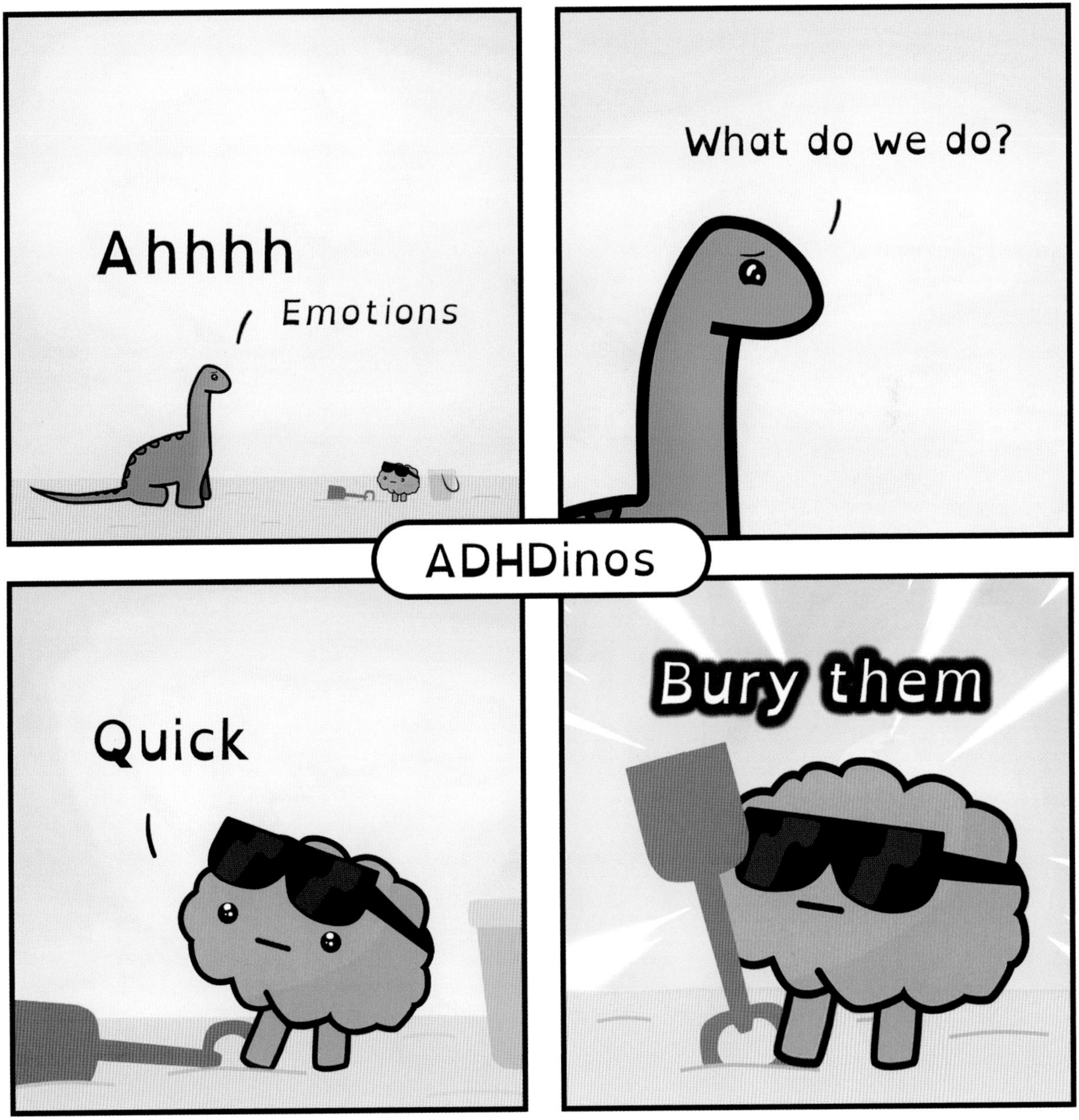
Ahhhh
Emotions
What do we do?
ADHDinos
Quick
Bury them

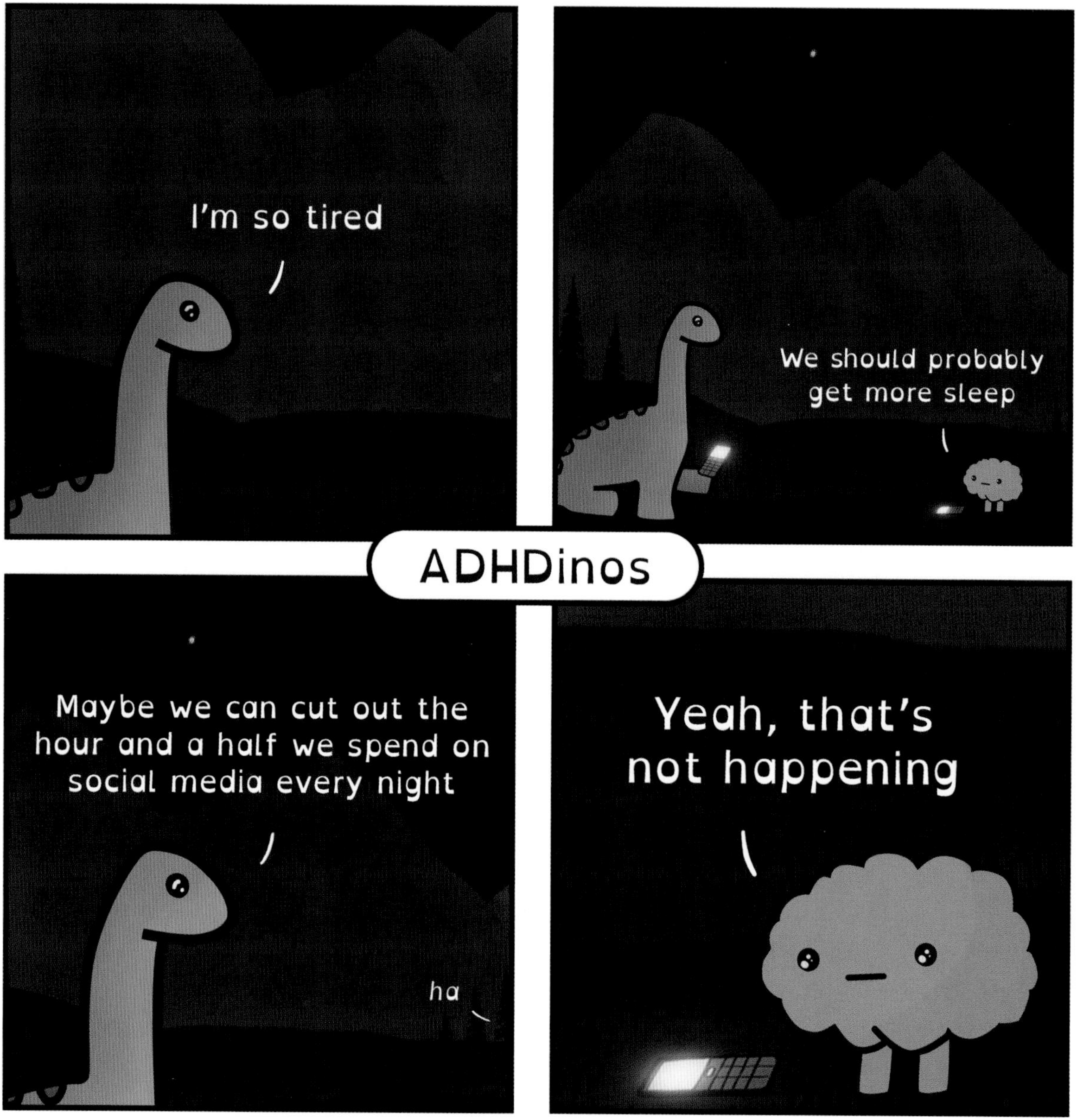
I'm so tired
We should probably get more sleep
ADHDinos
Maybe we can cut out the hour and a half we spend on social media every night
ha
Yeah, that's not happening

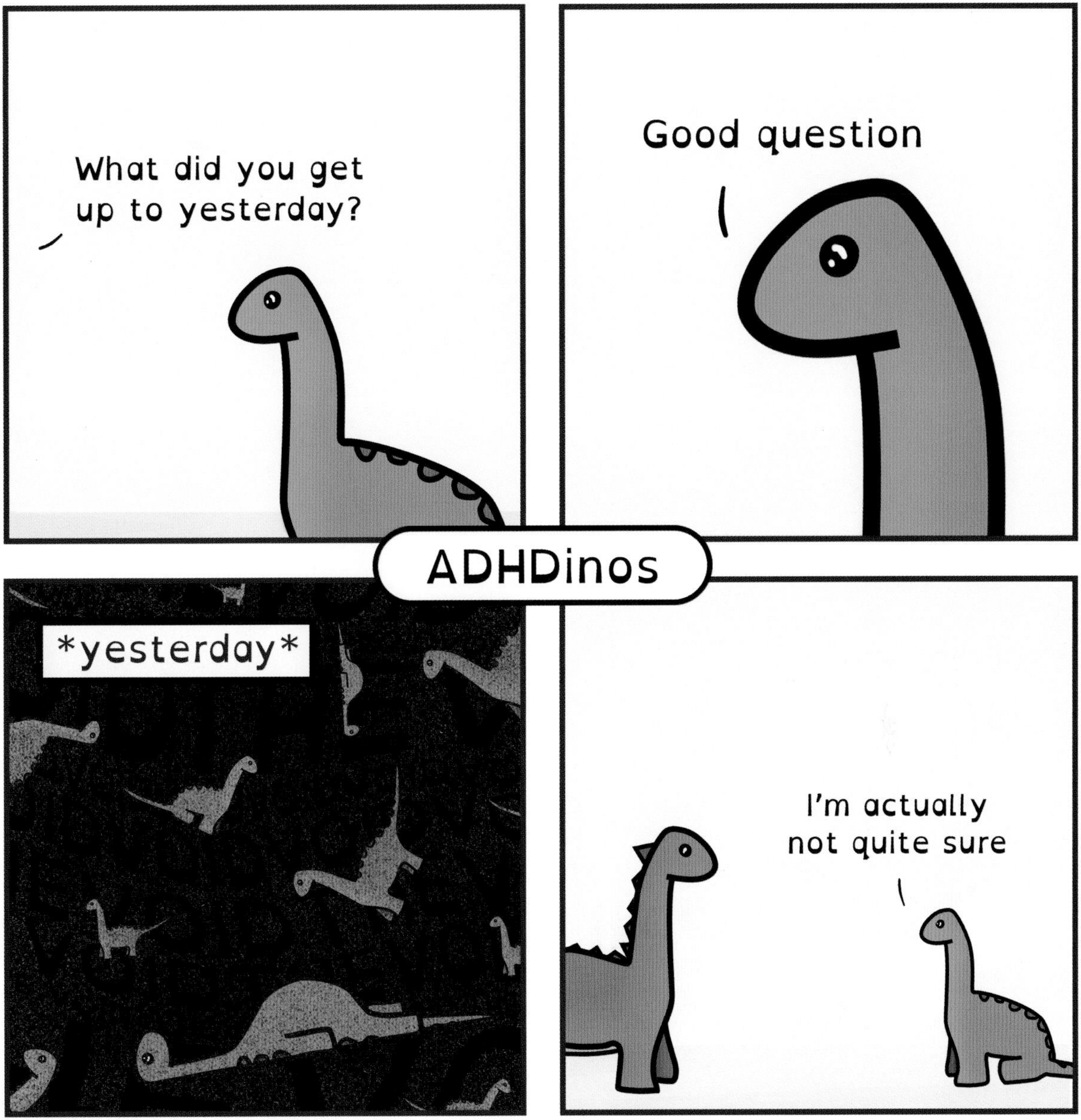
What did you get up to yesterday?
Good question
ADHDinos
yesterday
I'm actually not quite sure

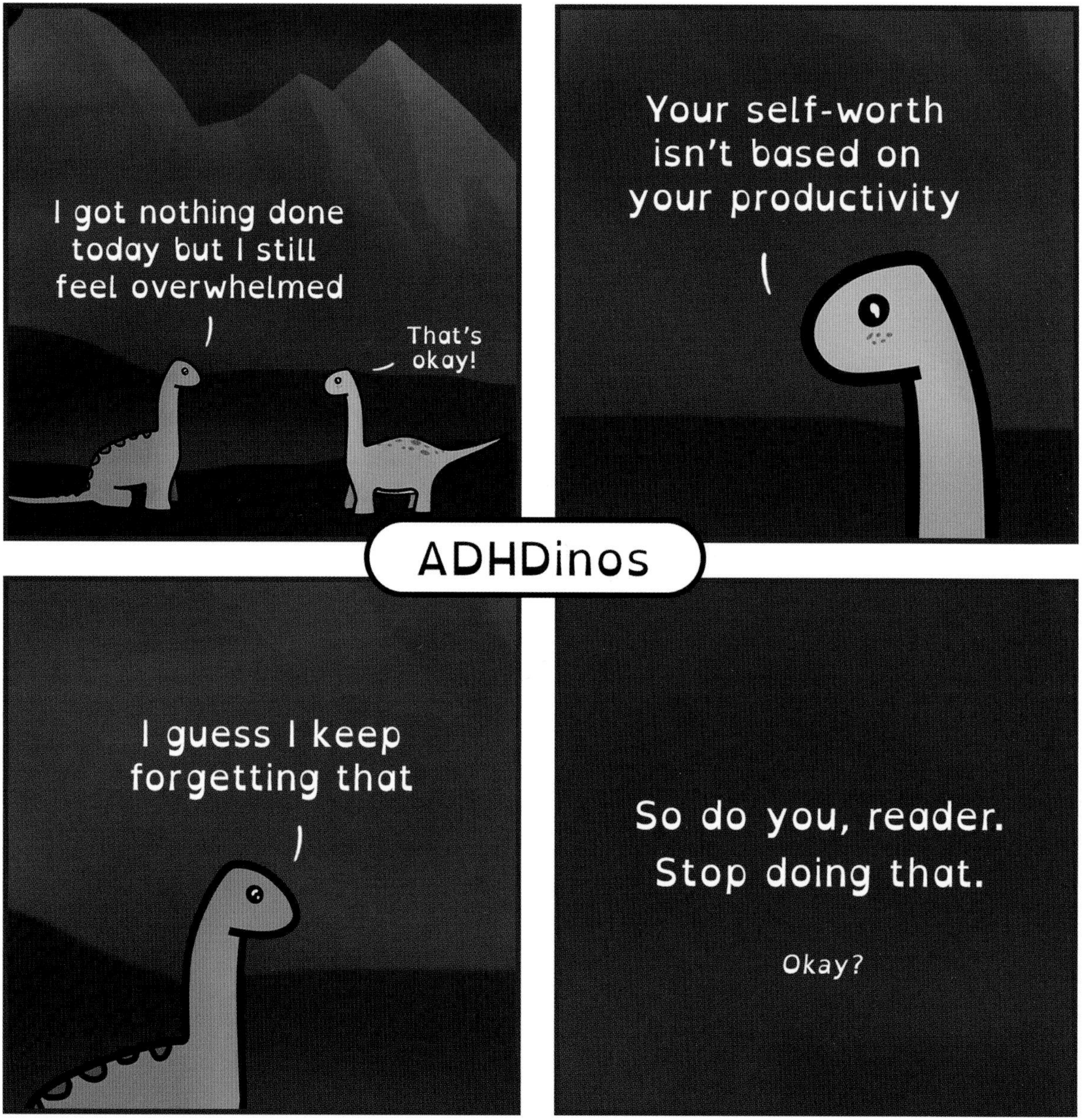
I got nothing done today but I still feel overwhelmed
That's okay!
Your self-worth isn't based on your productivity
ADHDinos
I guess I keep forgetting that
So do you, reader. Stop doing that.
Okay?

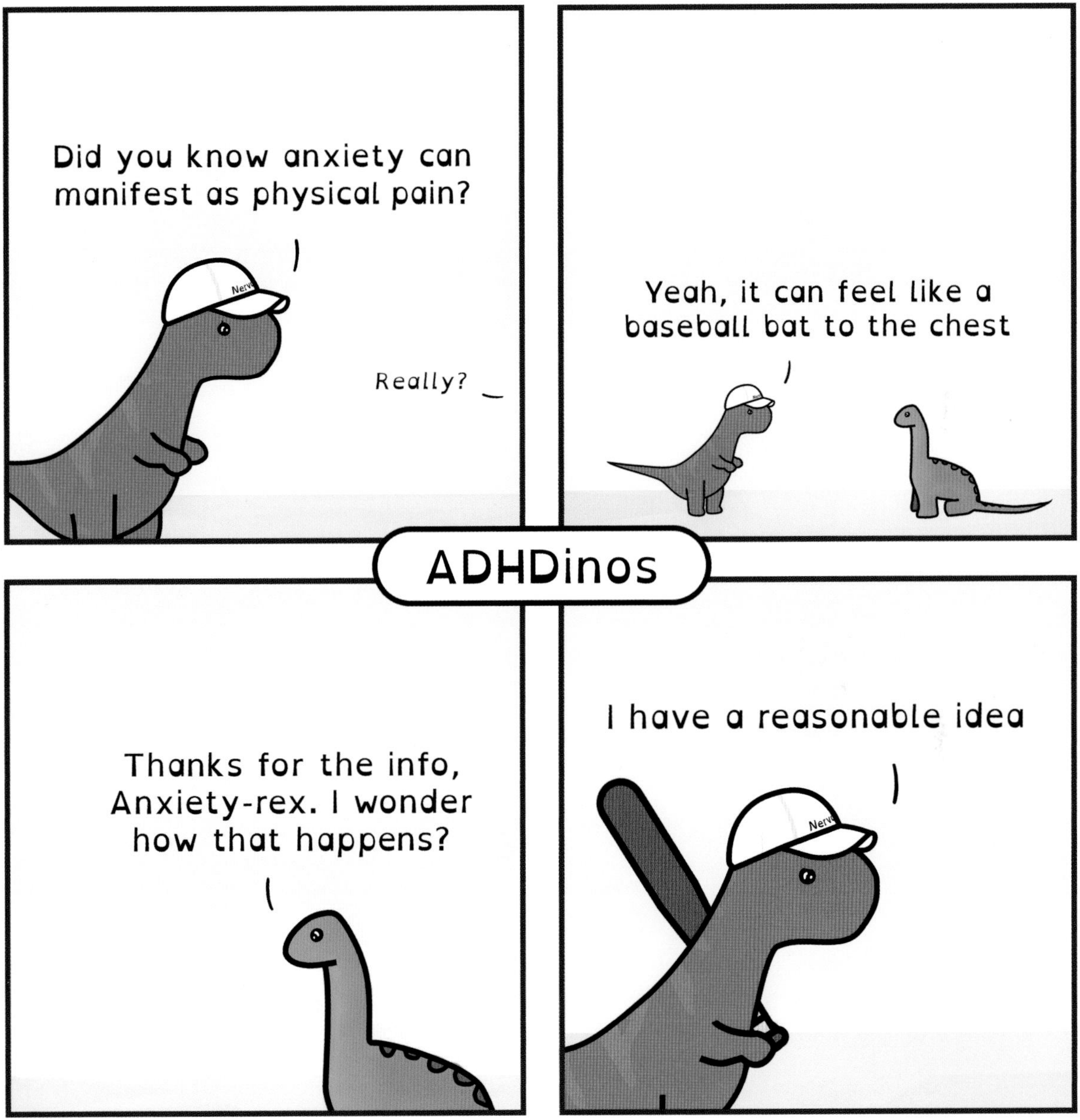

Did you know anxiety can manifest as physical pain?
Really?
Yeah, it can feel like a baseball bat to the chest
ADHDinos
Thanks for the info, Anxiety-rex. I wonder how that happens?
I have a reasonable idea

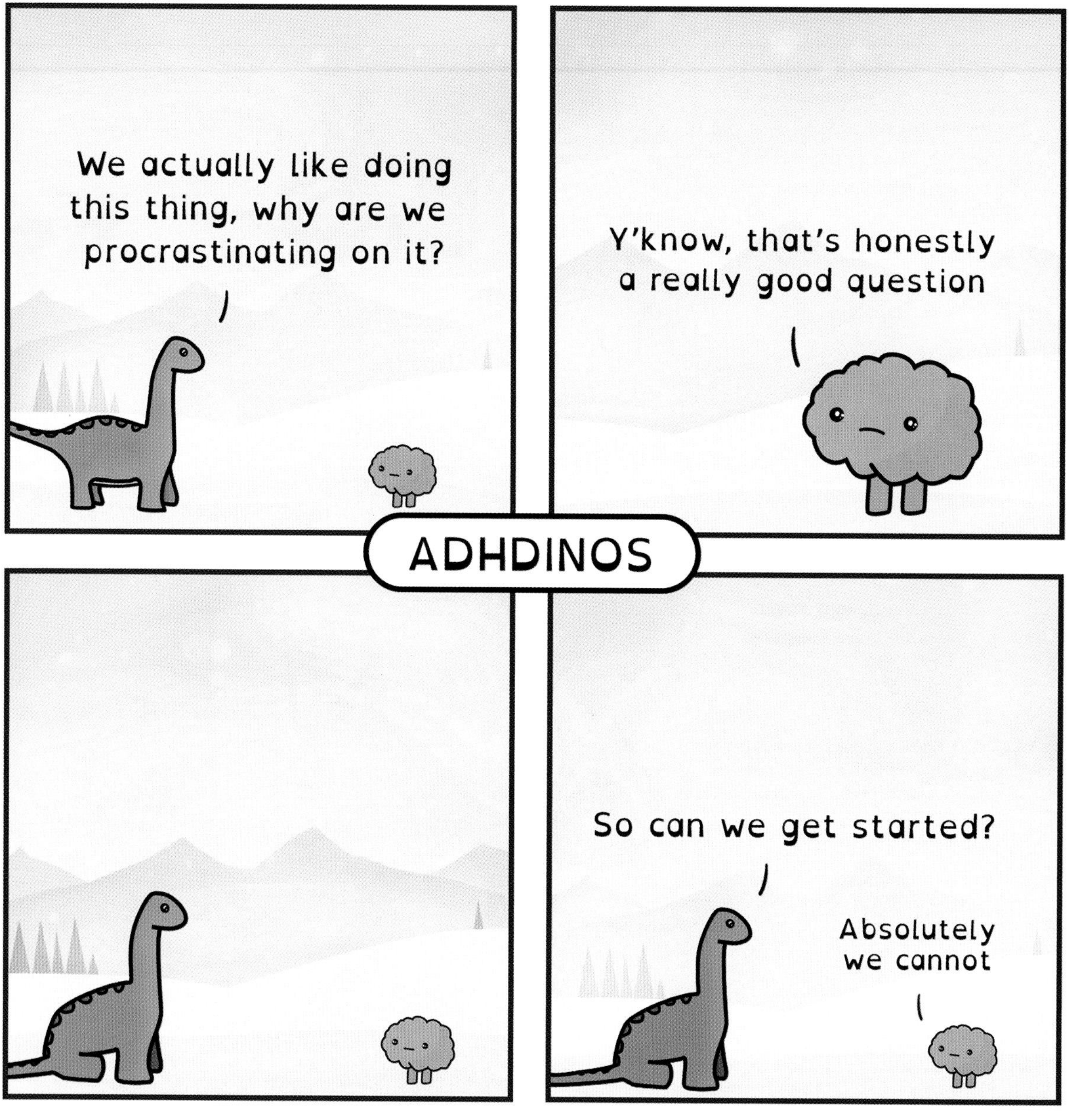
We actually like doing this thing, why are we procrastinating on it?
Y'know, that's honestly a really good question
ADHDINOS
So can we get started?
Absolutely we cannot

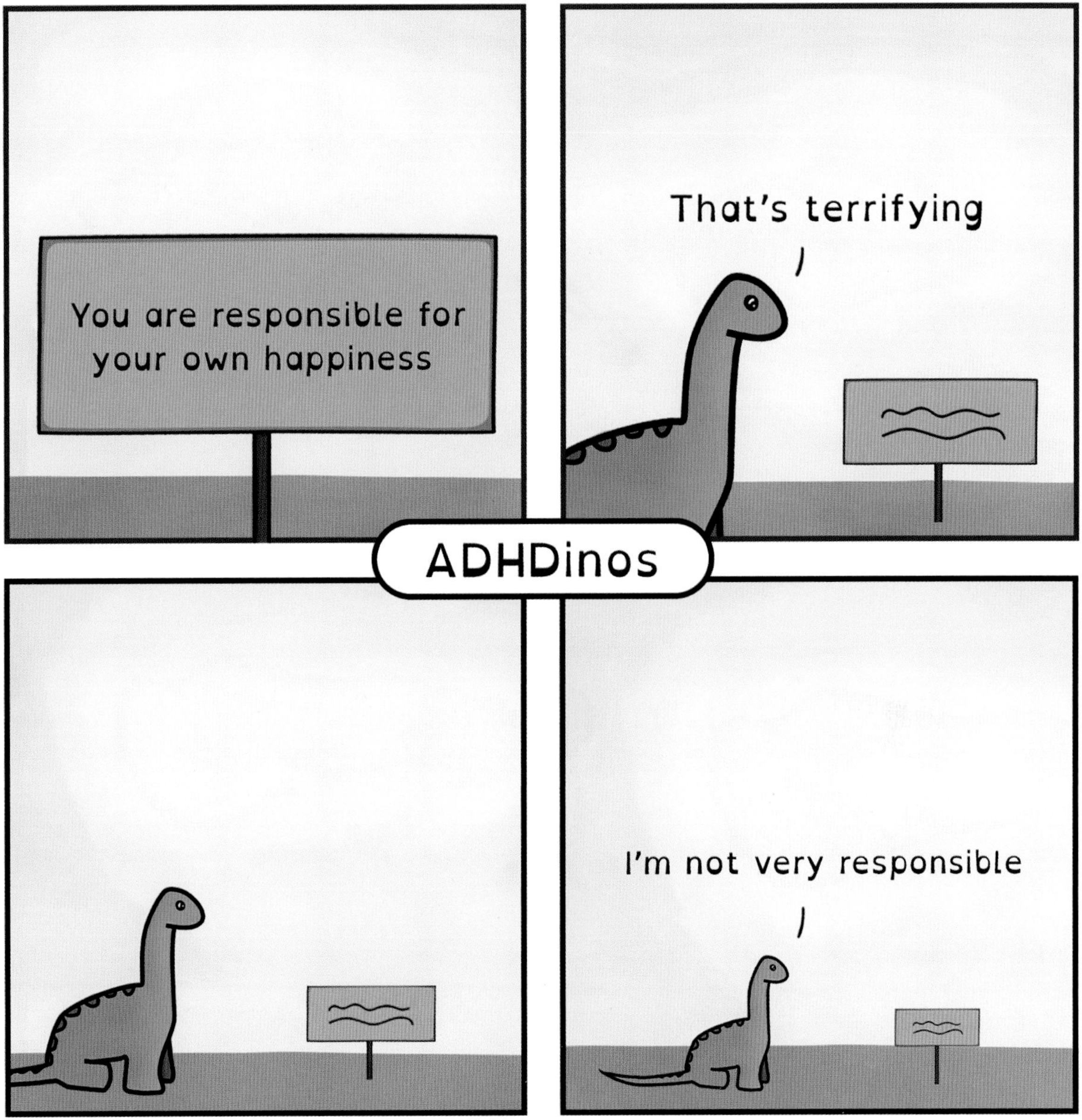
You are responsible for your own happiness
That's terrifying
ADHDinos
I'm not very responsible

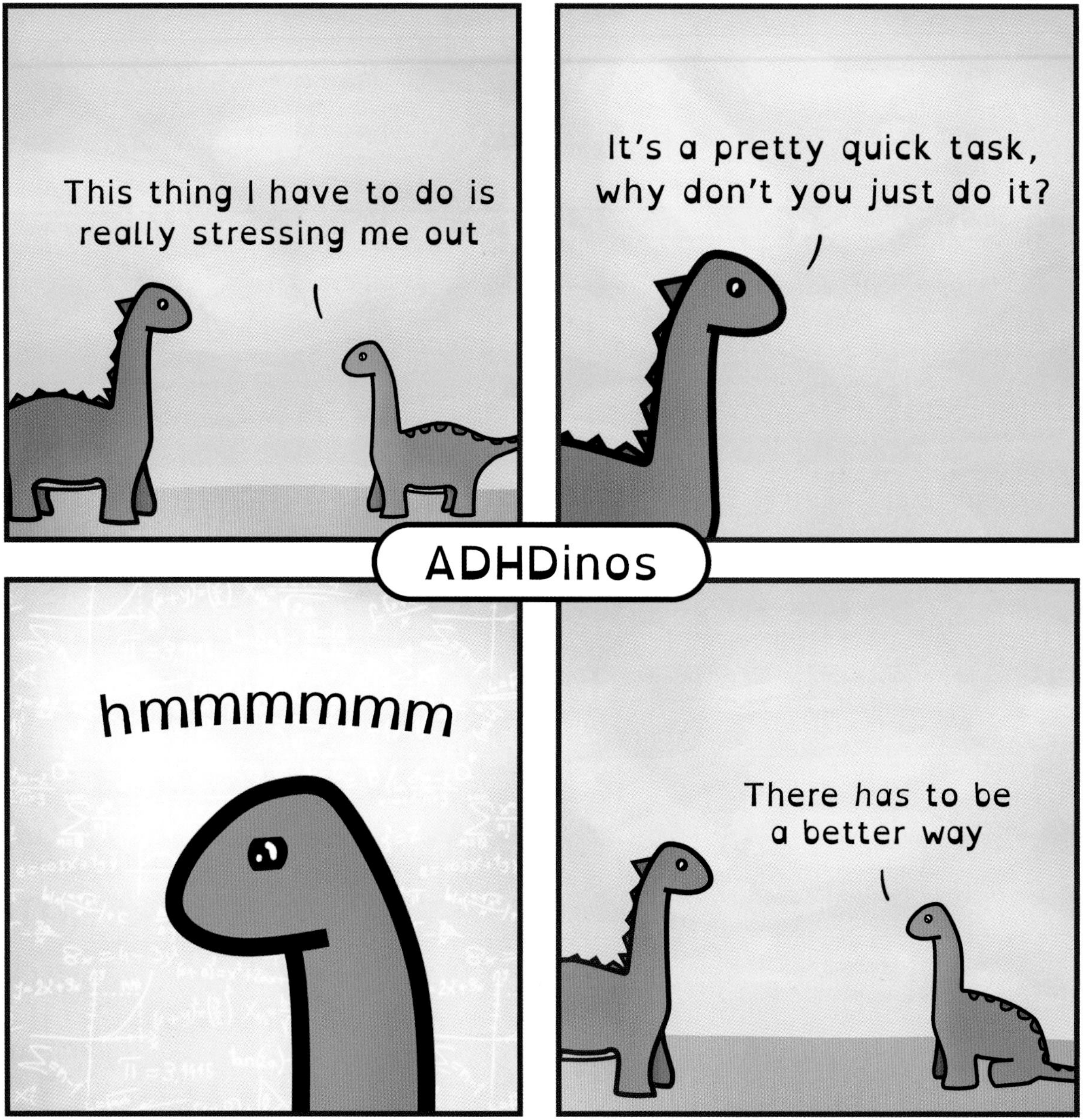
This thing I have to do is really stressing me out
It's a pretty quick task, why don't you just do it?
ADHDinos
hmmmmmmm
There *has* to be a better way

Executive Dysfunction

Individuals with ADHD struggle with executive functions that may otherwise come naturally to their peers. Those who struggle with executive dysfunction have more difficulty establishing and regulating goal-oriented behaviors. Executive dysfunction in those with ADHD can present itself as issues in time management, problem-solving, organization, procrastination, and planning, to name a few.

Most of the skills that comprise executive function can be practiced and improved upon. What helps someone overcome these issues varies greatly from individual to individual and requires a lot of effort, trial and error, and determination to develop and maintain (in other words, it can be really hard, but you can do it!).

Working from home was a productivity and logistical nightmare for Dino. Starting work felt hard. Doing work felt hard. And staying on track felt impossible. What eventually helped was creating a designated workspace and following very specific start and stop times, but this took a considerable amount of time to learn.

As with anything, progress can be slow (or sometimes seemingly nonexistent), but it's important to remember that all progress is progress. Things do eventually click, even if it sometimes feels like they never will. Progress often comes in leaps and bounds, especially when you're not measuring it so critically. It's really important to set reasonable, manageable goals and recognize your successes.

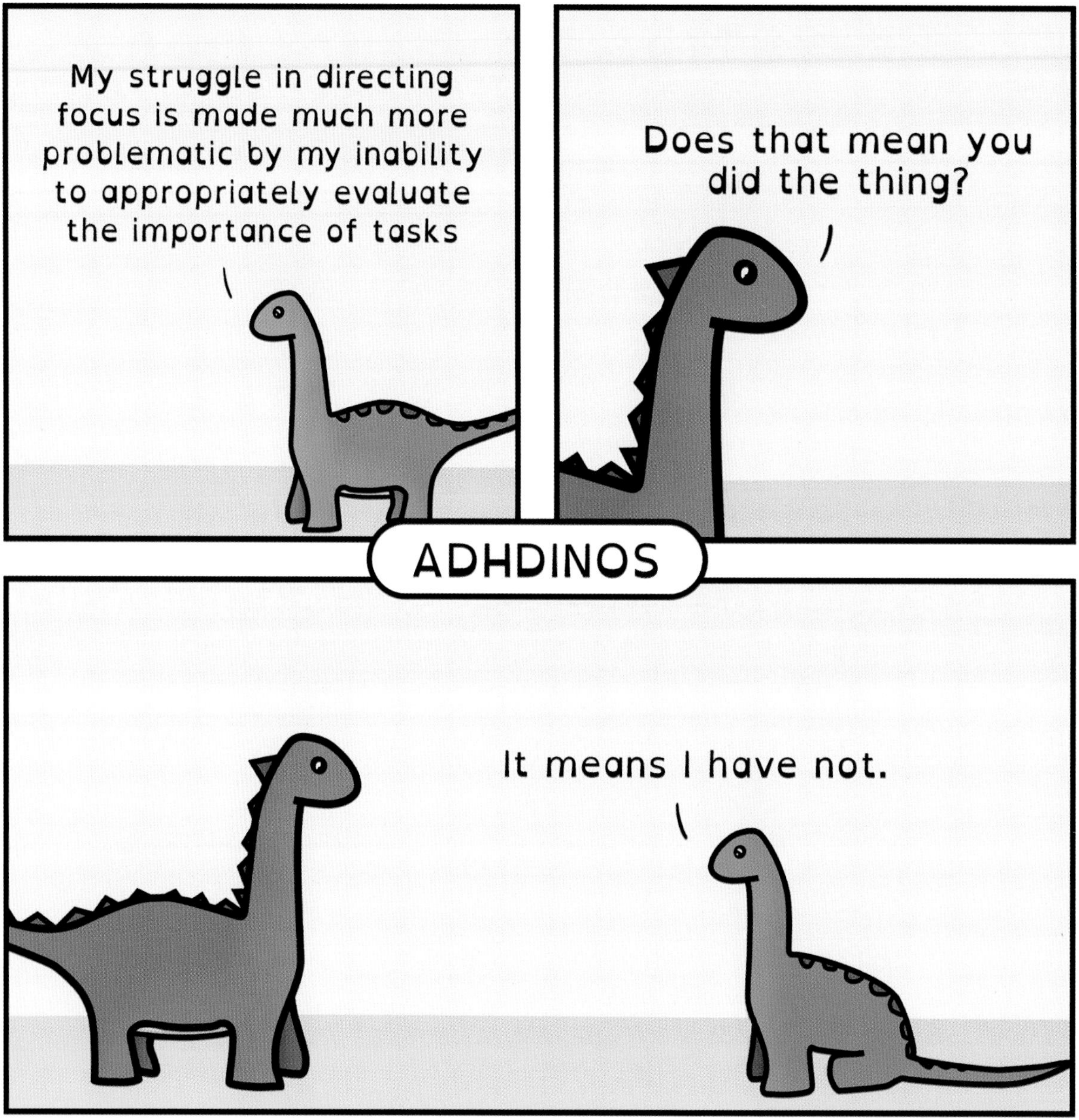
My struggle in directing focus is made much more problematic by my inability to appropriately evaluate the importance of tasks
Does that mean you did the thing?
ADHDINOS
It means I have not.

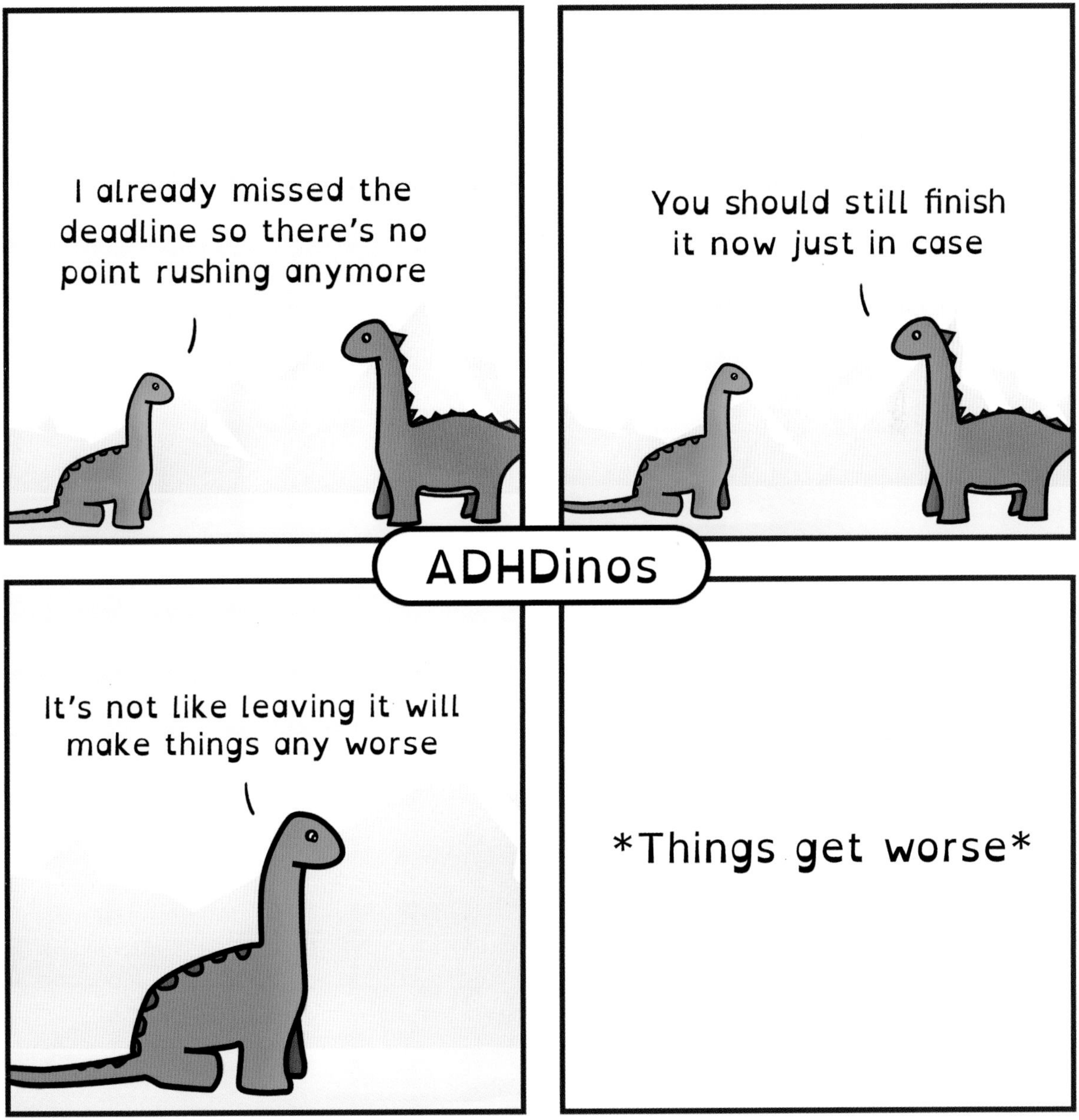
I already missed the deadline so there's no point rushing anymore
You should still finish it now just in case
ADHDinos
It's not like leaving it will make things any worse
Things get worse

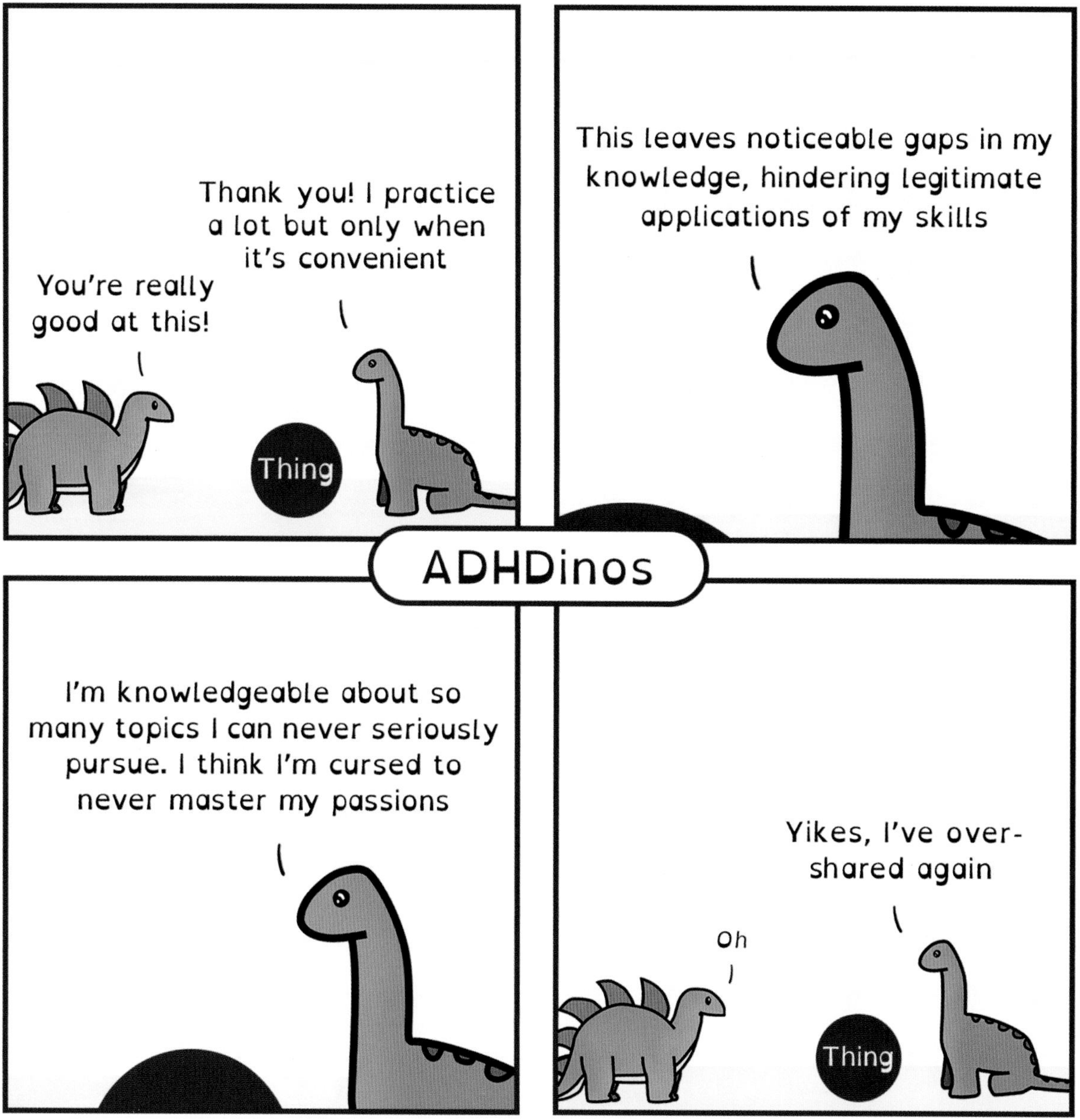
ADHDinos
You're really good at this!
Thank you! I practice a lot but only when it's convenient
Thing
This leaves noticeable gaps in my knowledge, hindering legitimate applications of my skills
I'm knowledgeable about so many topics I can never seriously pursue. I think I'm cursed to never master my passions
Oh
Yikes, I've over-shared again
Thing

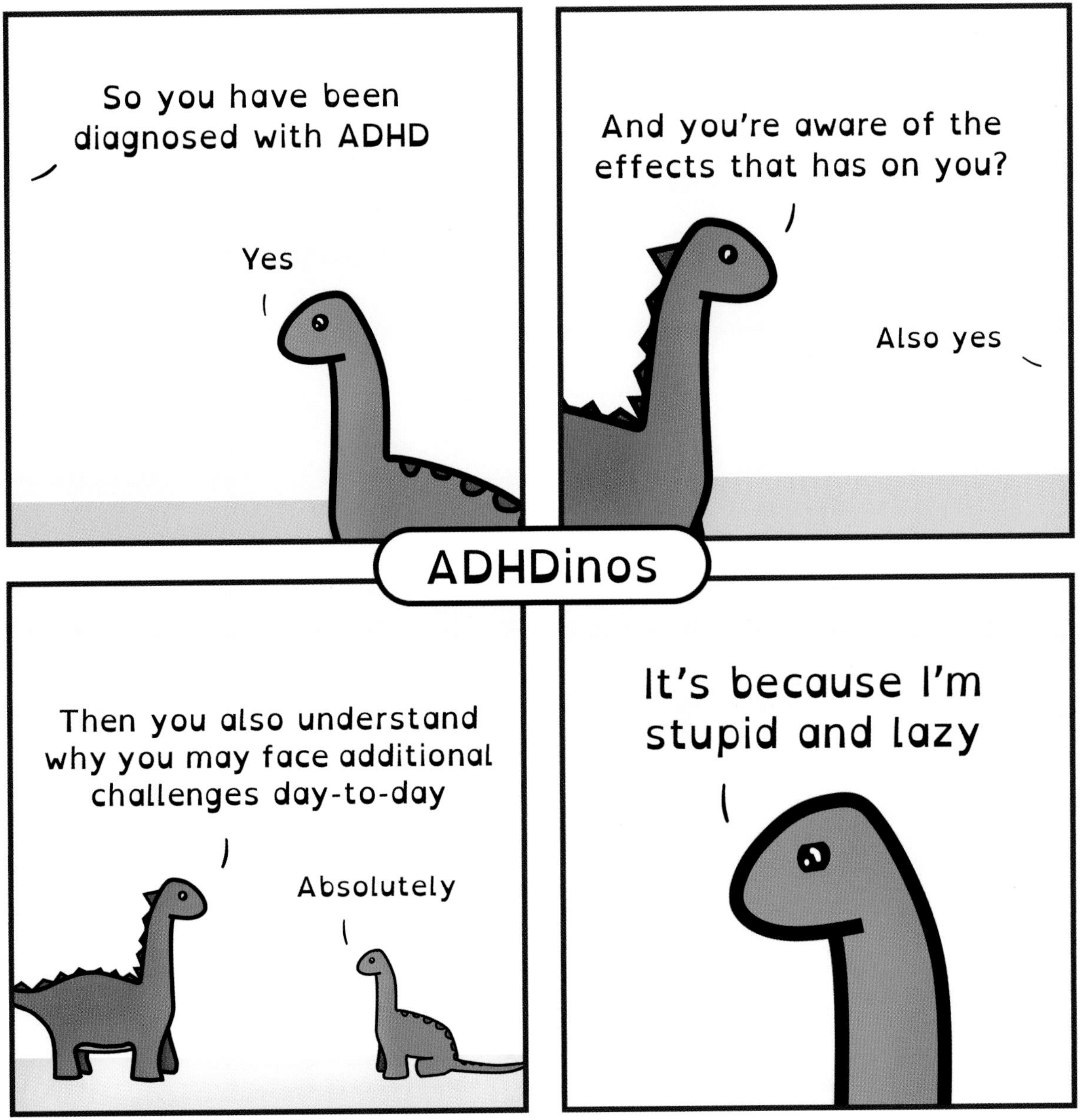
So you have been diagnosed with ADHD
Yes
And you're aware of the effects that has on you?
Also yes
ADHDinos
Then you also understand why you may face additional challenges day-to-day
Absolutely
It's because I'm stupid and lazy

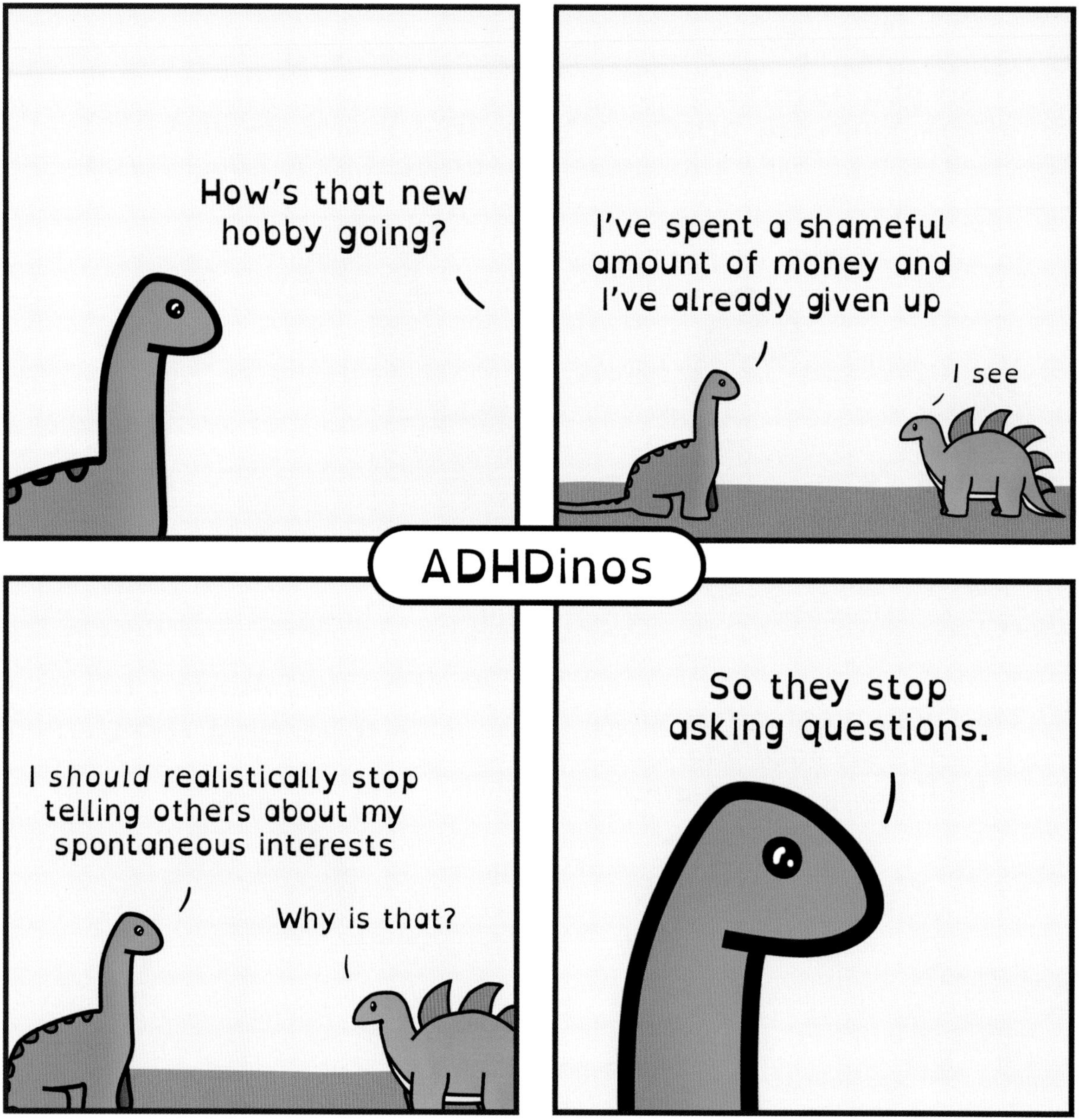
How's that new hobby going?
I've spent a shameful amount of money and I've already given up
I see
ADHDinos
I *should* realistically stop telling others about my spontaneous interests
Why is that?
So they stop asking questions.

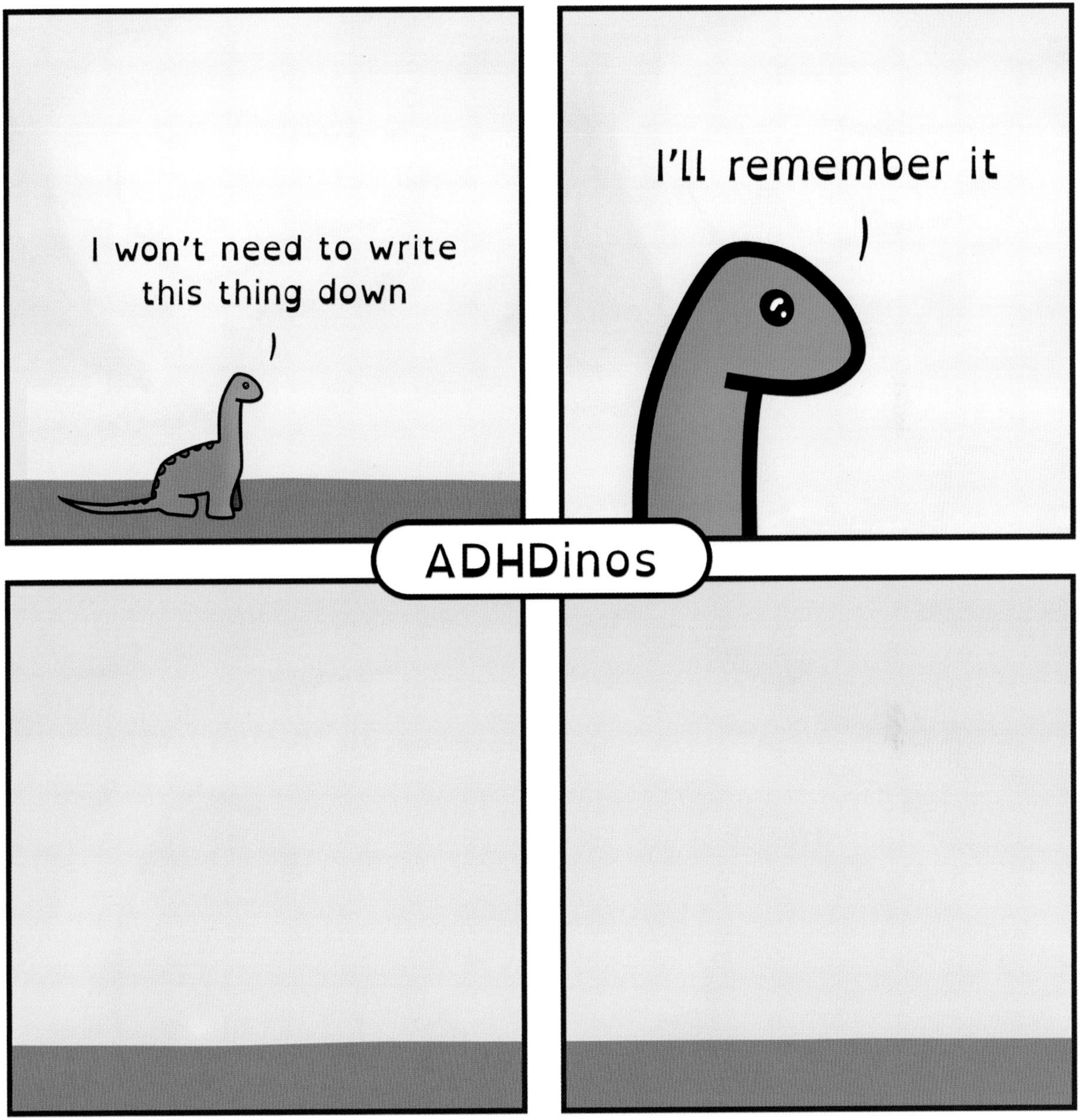
I won't need to write this thing down
I'll remember it
ADHDinos

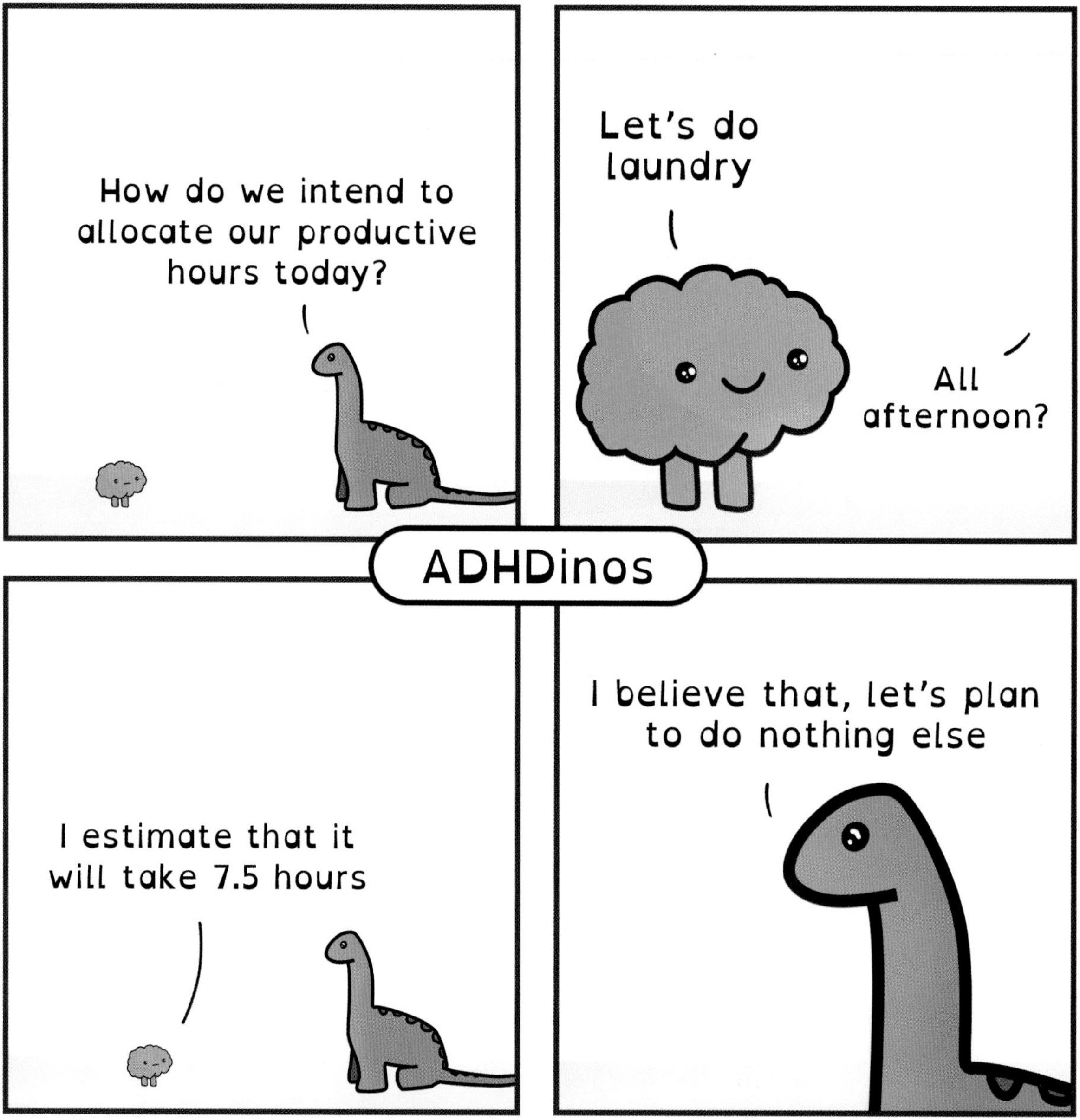
How do we intend to allocate our productive hours today?
Let's do laundry
All afternoon?
ADHDinos
I estimate that it will take 7.5 hours
I believe that, let's plan to do nothing else

"Time Blindness"

People with ADHD have more trouble perceiving and predicting the passing of time, something often referred to as time blindness.[*] Time blindness causes difficulties with planning, adhering to deadlines, recounting events, and remembering tasks—to name a few.

When planning ahead, Dino will often greatly over- or underestimate the importance of tasks and the time required for them, which leaves him stressed about nothing or scrambling at the last minute. Planning out full days and adhering to schedules is often very difficult for this reason.

[*] Ptacek, R., Weissenberger, S., Braaten, E.B., Klicperova-Baker, M., Goetz, M., Raboch, J., Vnukova, M., & Stefano, G.B. Clinical implications of the perception of time in attention deficit hyperactivity disorder (ADHD): a review. *Medical Science Monitor* 25, 3918-3924 (May 2019). https://www.researchgate.net/publication/333392307_Clinical_Implications_of_the_Perception_of_Time_in_Attention_Deficit_Hyperactivity_Disorder_ADHD_A_Review

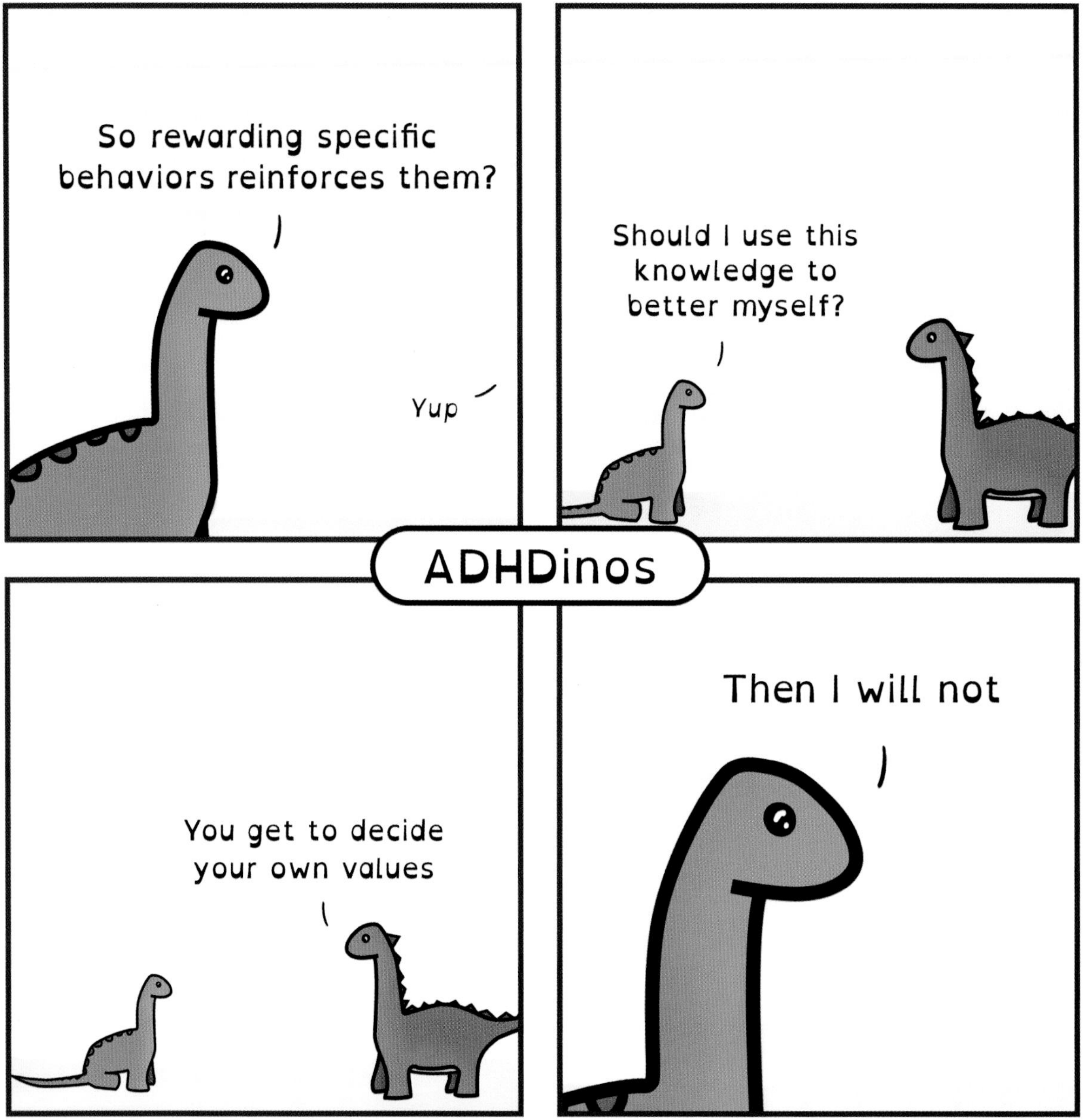
So rewarding specific behaviors reinforces them?
Yup
Should I use this knowledge to better myself?
ADHDinos
You get to decide your own values
Then I will not

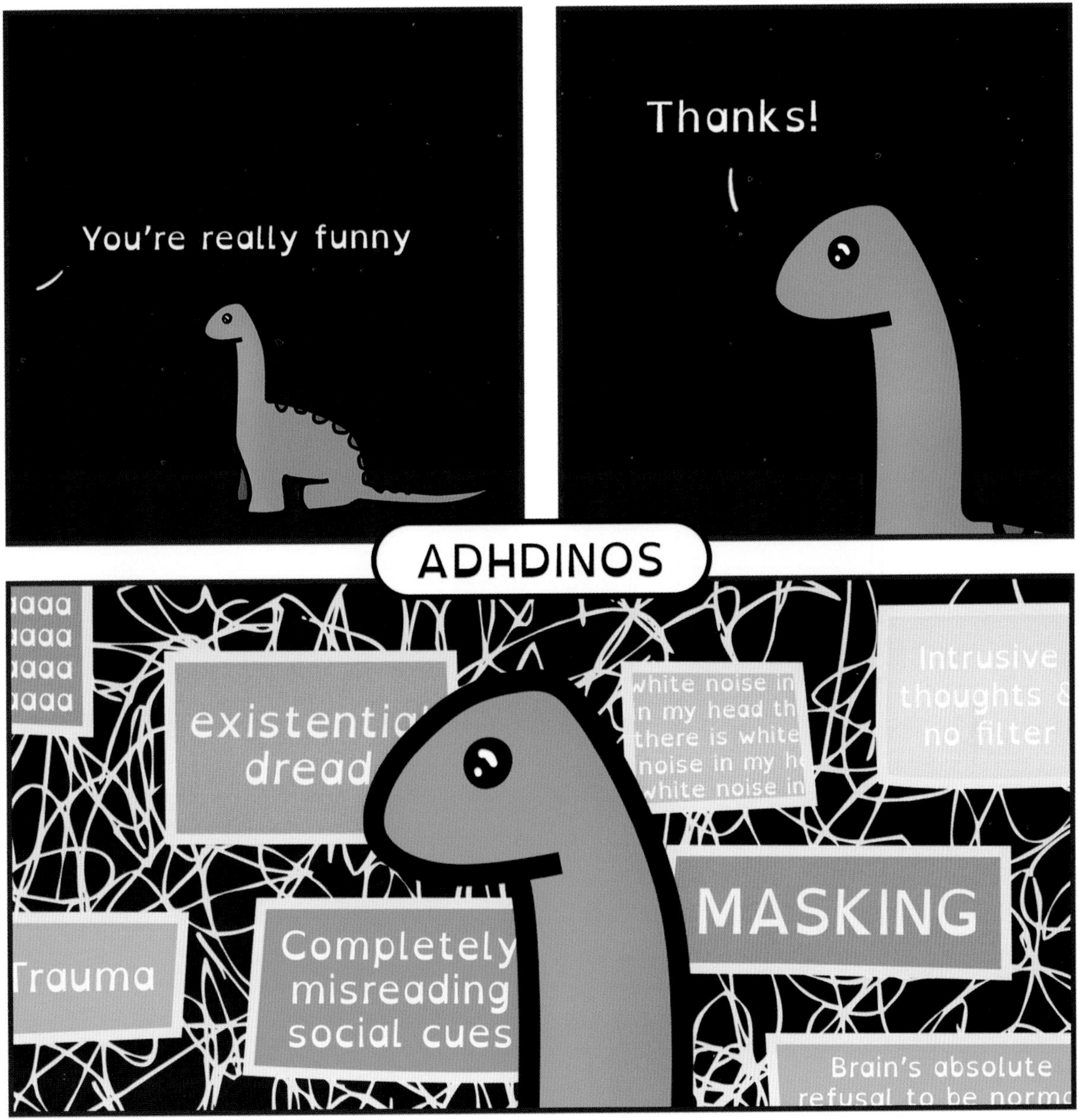
You're really funny
Thanks!
ADHDINOS
aaaa
aaaa
aaaa
aaaa
existential dread
white noise in
in my head th
there is white
noise in my h
white noise in
Intrusive thoughts & no filter
MASKING
Trauma
Completely misreading social cues
Brain's absolute refusal to be norm

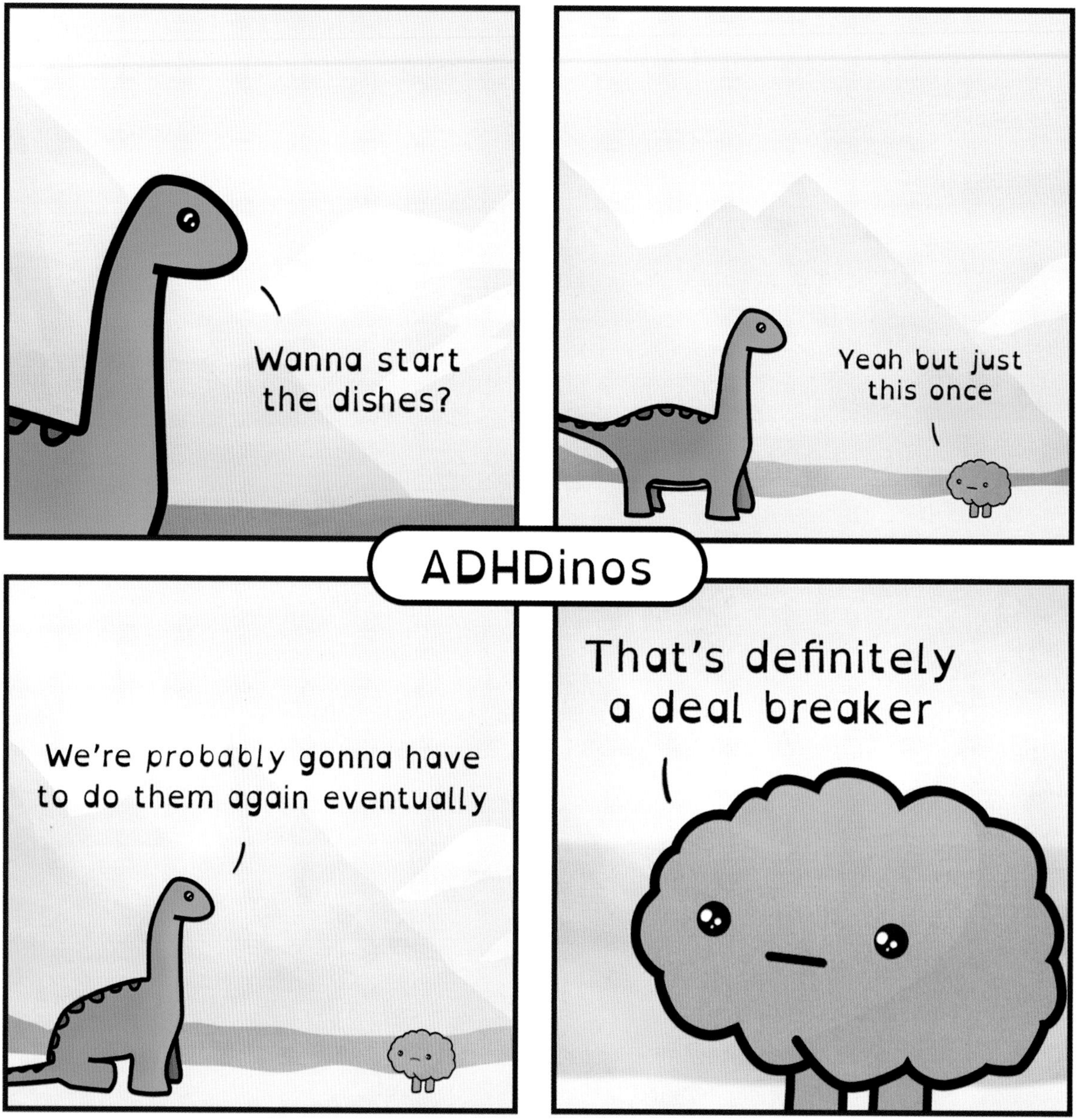
ADHDinos
Wanna start the dishes?
Yeah but just this once
We're *probably* gonna have to do them again eventually
That's definitely a deal breaker

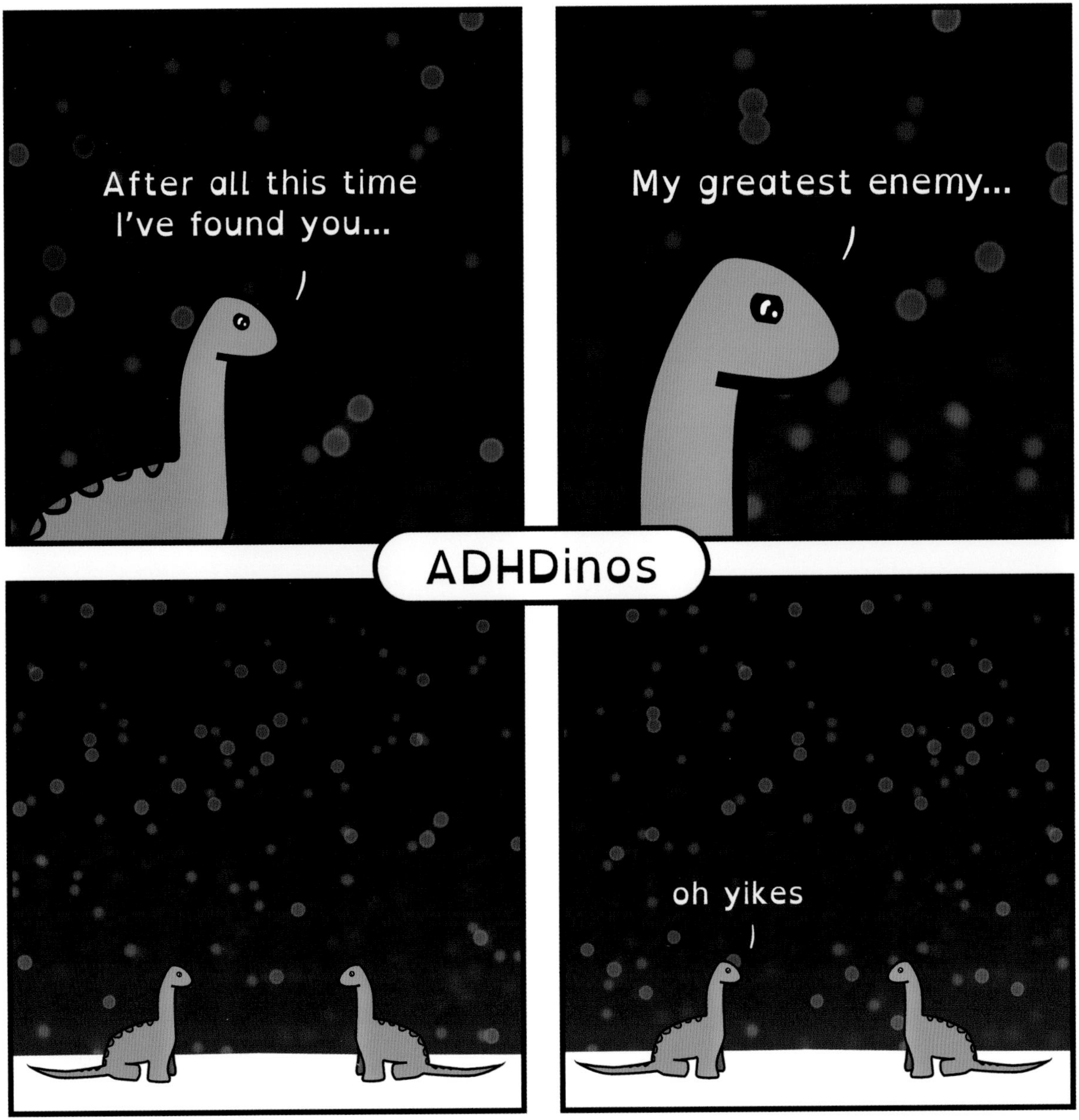
After all this time
I've found you...
My greatest enemy...
ADHDinos
oh yikes

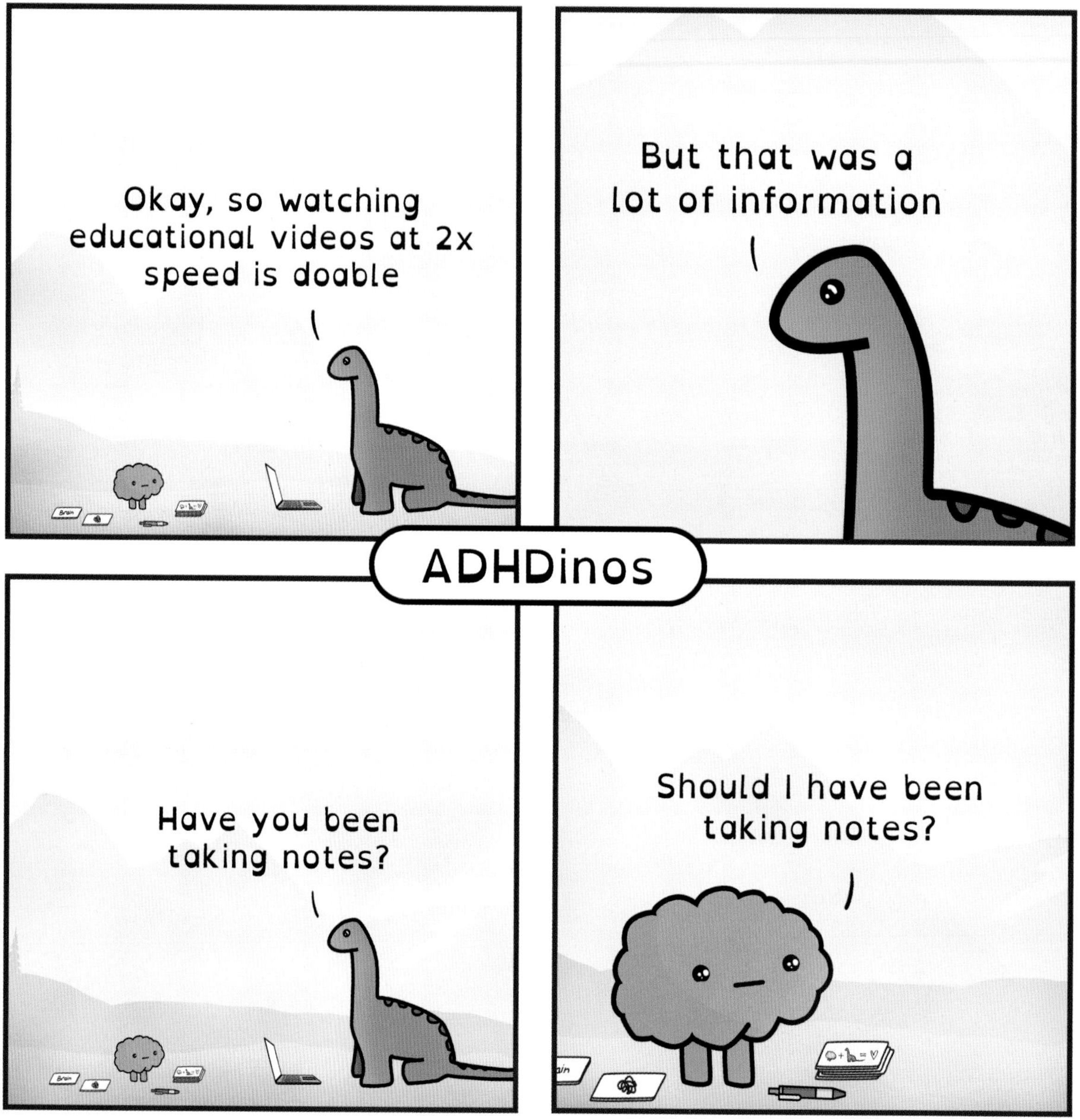
Okay, so watching educational videos at 2x speed is doable
But that was a lot of information
ADHDinos
Have you been taking notes?
Should I have been taking notes?

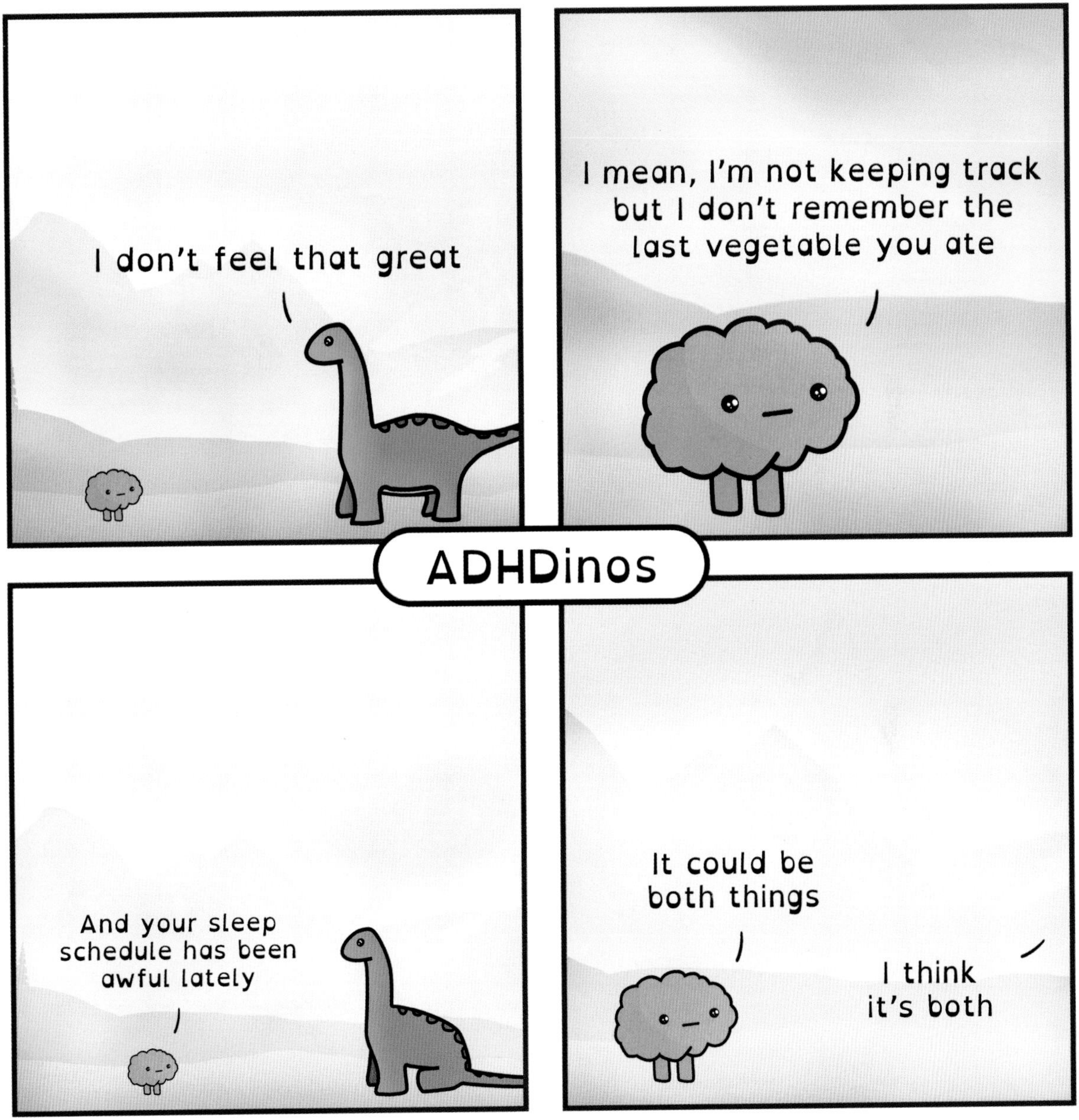
I don't feel that great
I mean, I'm not keeping track but I don't remember the last vegetable you ate
ADHDinos
And your sleep schedule has been awful lately
It could be both things
I think it's both

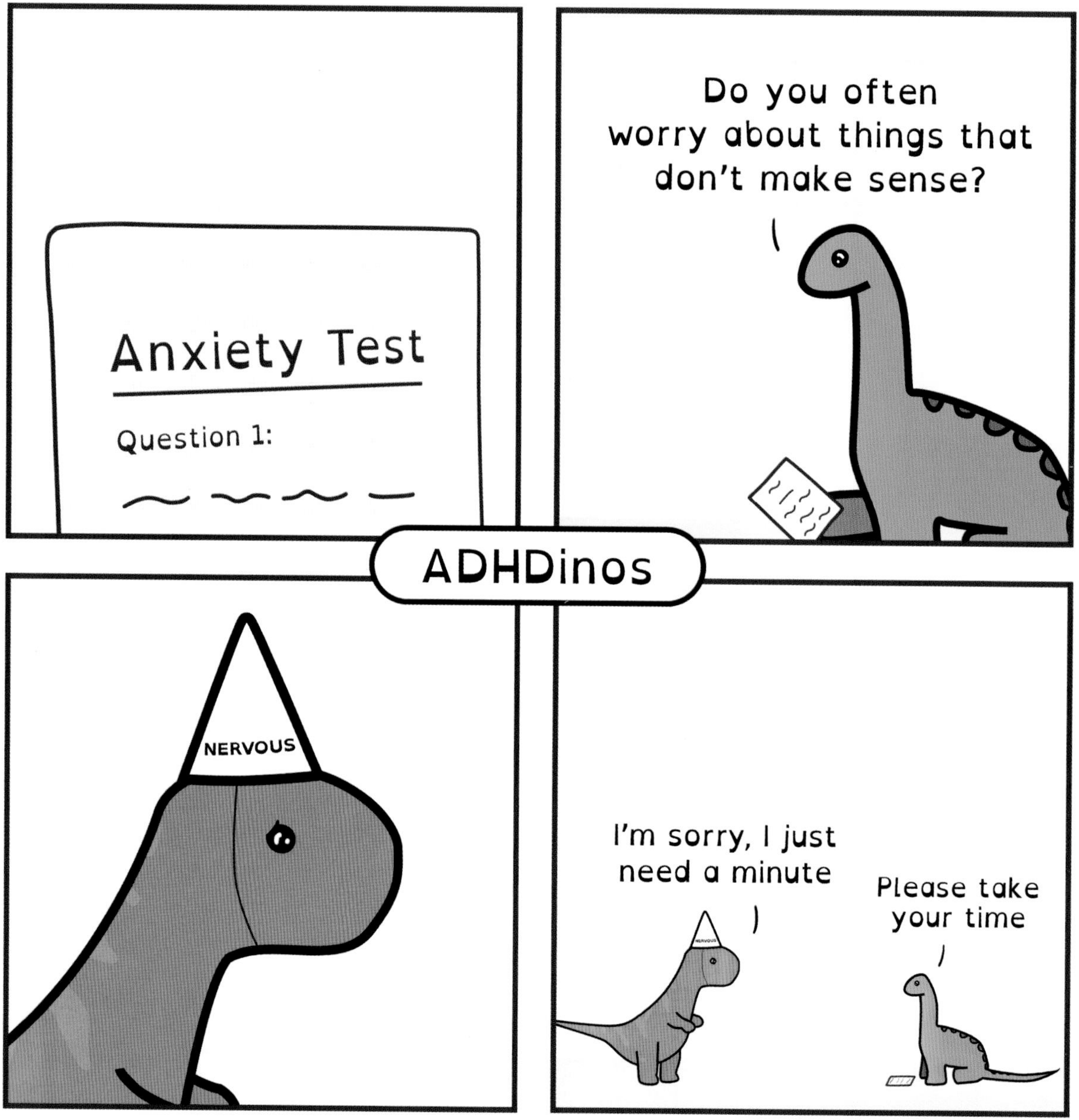

Anxiety Test
Question 1:
Do you often worry about things that don't make sense?
ADHDinos
NERVOUS
I'm sorry, I just need a minute
Please take your time

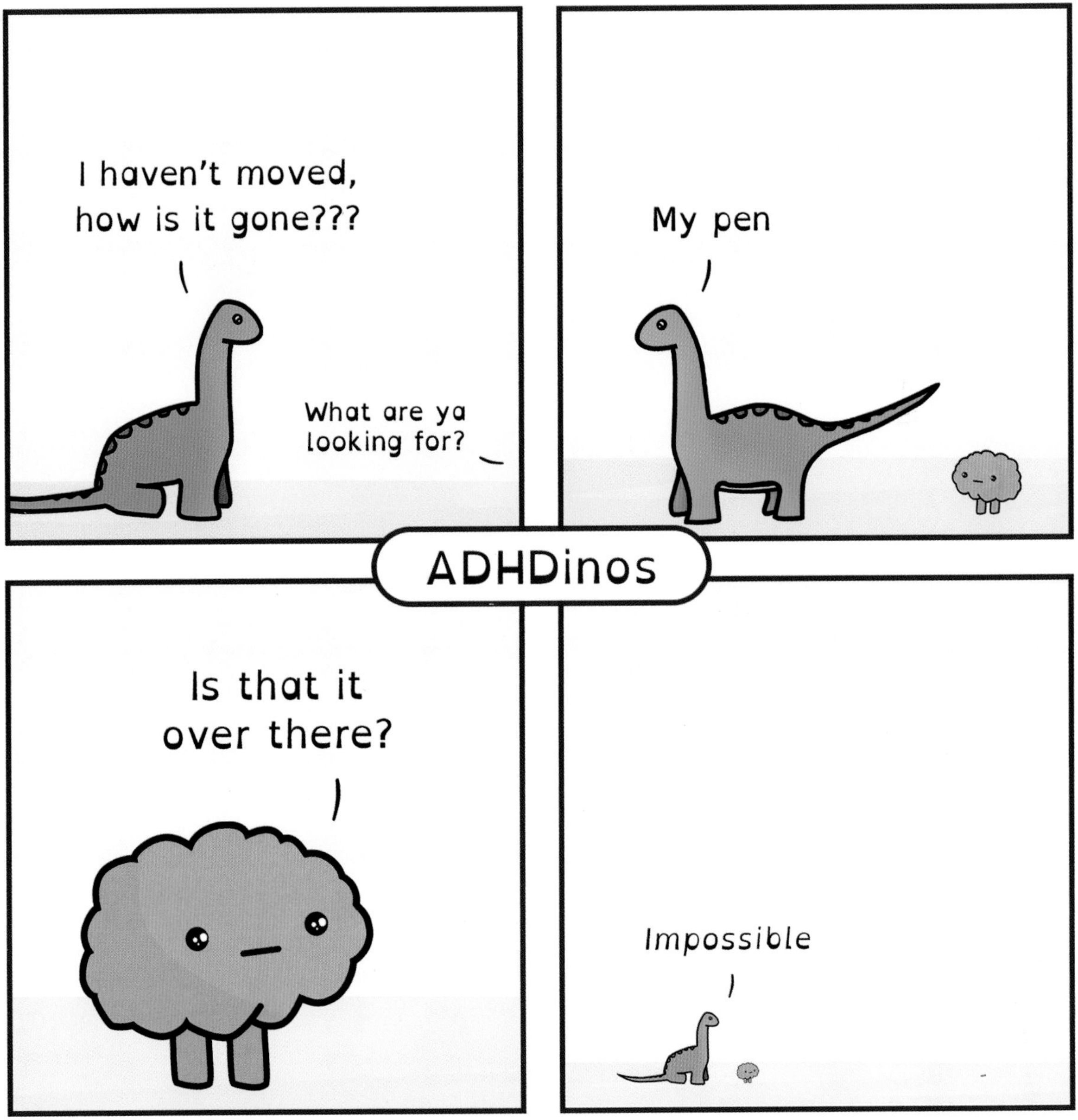
What are ya looking for?
I haven't moved, how is it gone???
My pen
ADHDinos
Is that it over there?
Impossible

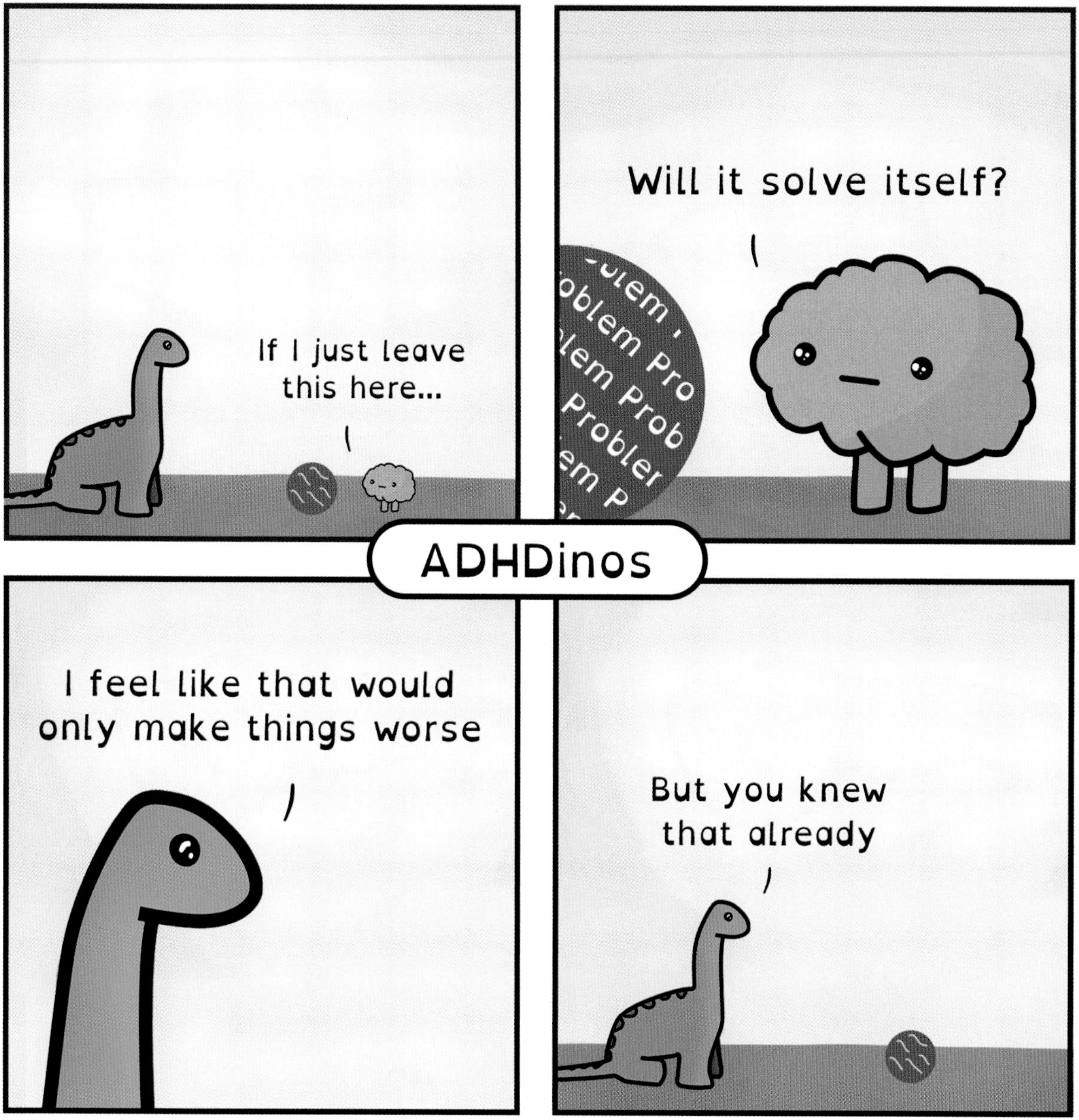
If I just leave this here...
Will it solve itself?
ADHDinos
I feel like that would only make things worse
But you knew that already

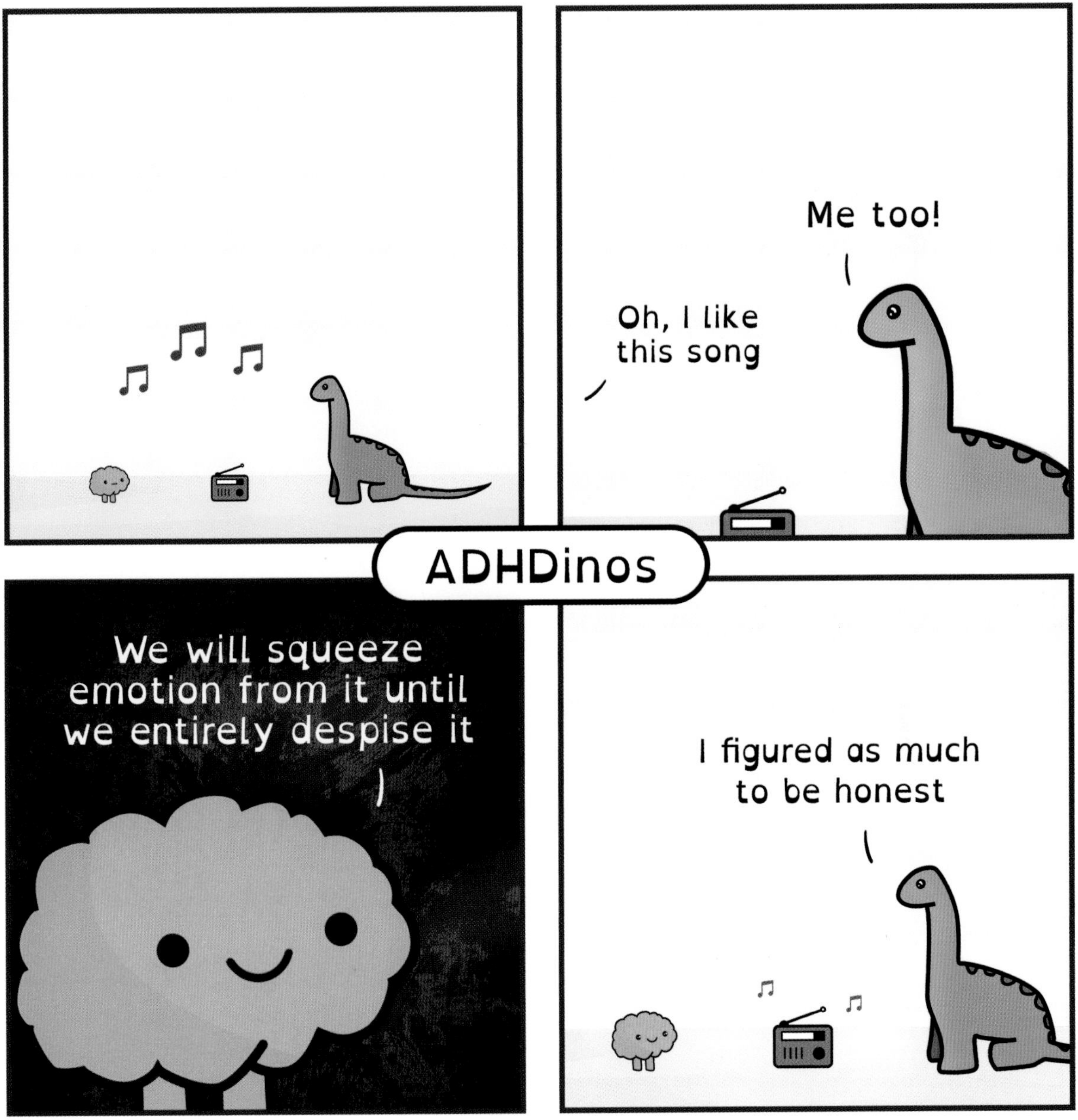
Oh, I like this song
Me too!
ADHDinos
We will squeeze emotion from it until we entirely despise it
I figured as much to be honest

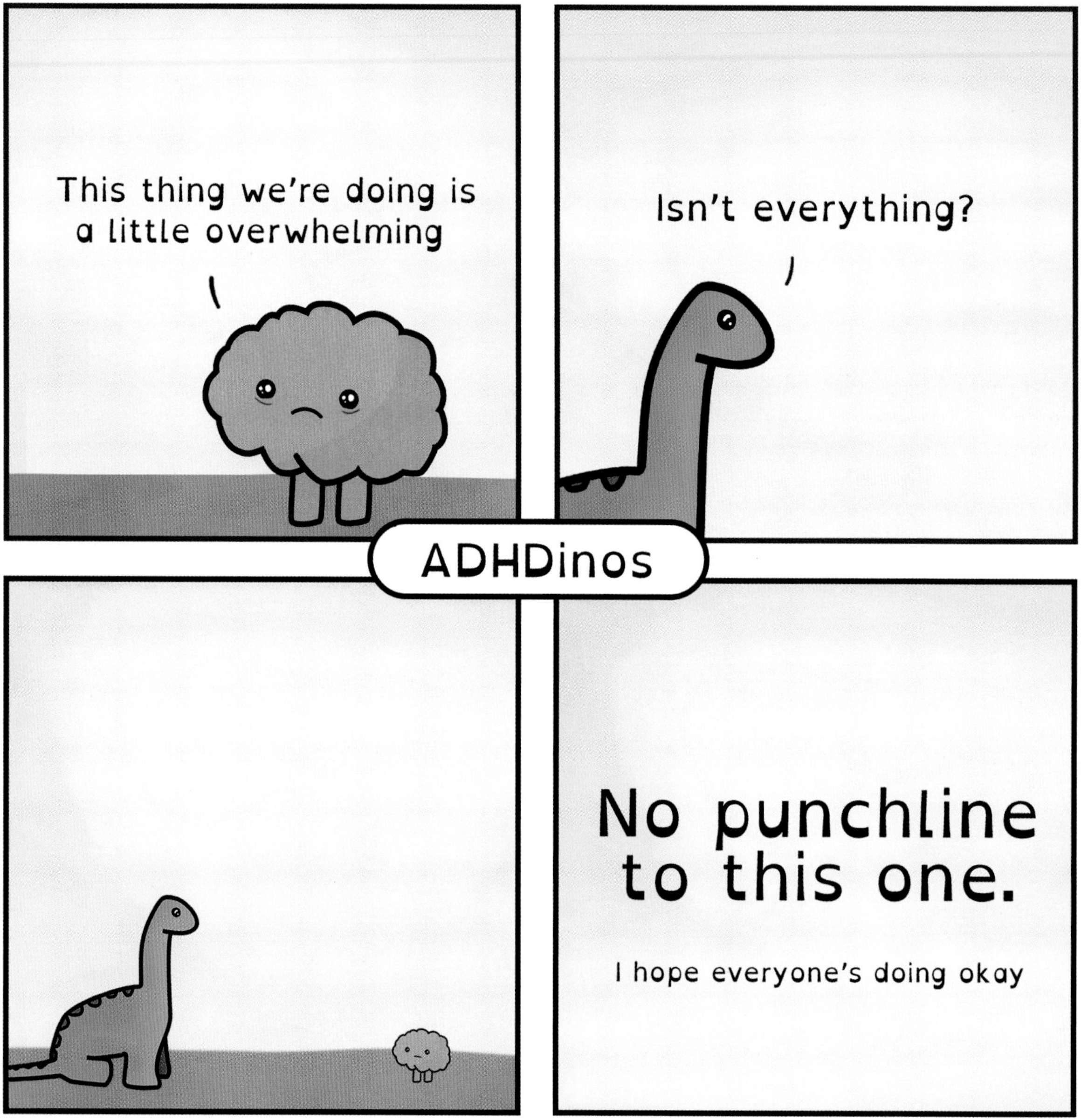
This thing we're doing is a little overwhelming
Isn't everything?
ADHDinos
No punchline to this one.
I hope everyone's doing okay

Burnout

Sometimes people push themselves too far, and there's no shame in that. Burnout—the physical, emotional, and mental exhaustion that results from ongoing stress—can be caused by untreated symptoms of ADHD and the unhealthy coping mechanisms one may develop to deal with them on their own. Signs of burnout include **anxiety**, detachment, lack of sleep, and lack of motivation, but all diagnoses should start with a conversation with a medical professional.

Burnout is usually the body's way of saying it can't keep going on as it is. Some issues can get so big that they feel like they're more important than your mental and physical well-being, but that's pretty much never the case. In the heat of burnout, it can be really difficult to identify that you're struggling before the situation becomes too much to handle.

Dino sometimes feels like he's being pulled in every direction by everyone. Ultimately, if he's bitten off more than he can chew, he either has to step back and approach the issues he's facing differently or relinquish some responsibilities. He's only one Dino.

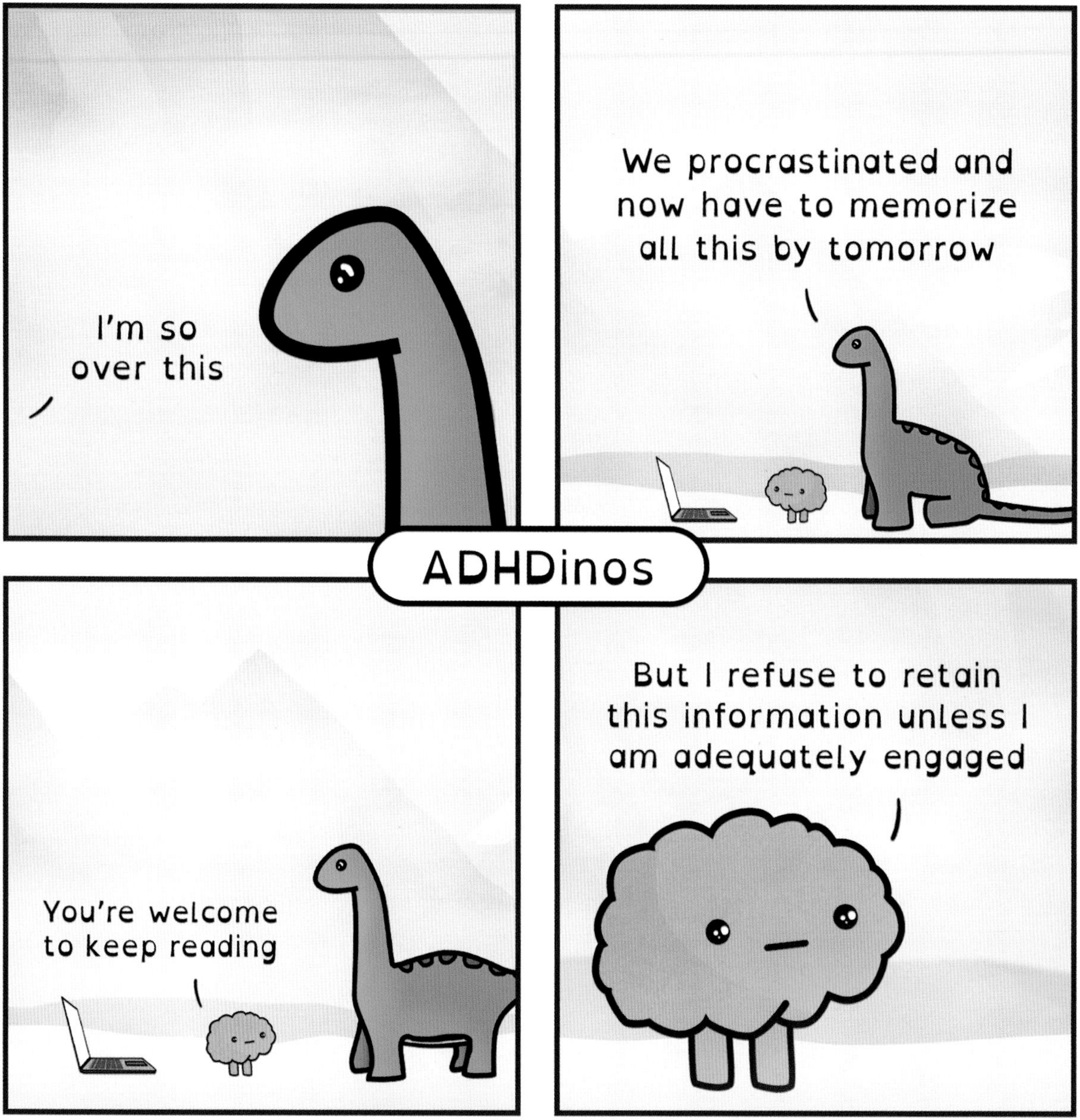
I'm so over this
We procrastinated and now have to memorize all this by tomorrow
ADHDinos
You're welcome to keep reading
But I refuse to retain this information unless I am adequately engaged

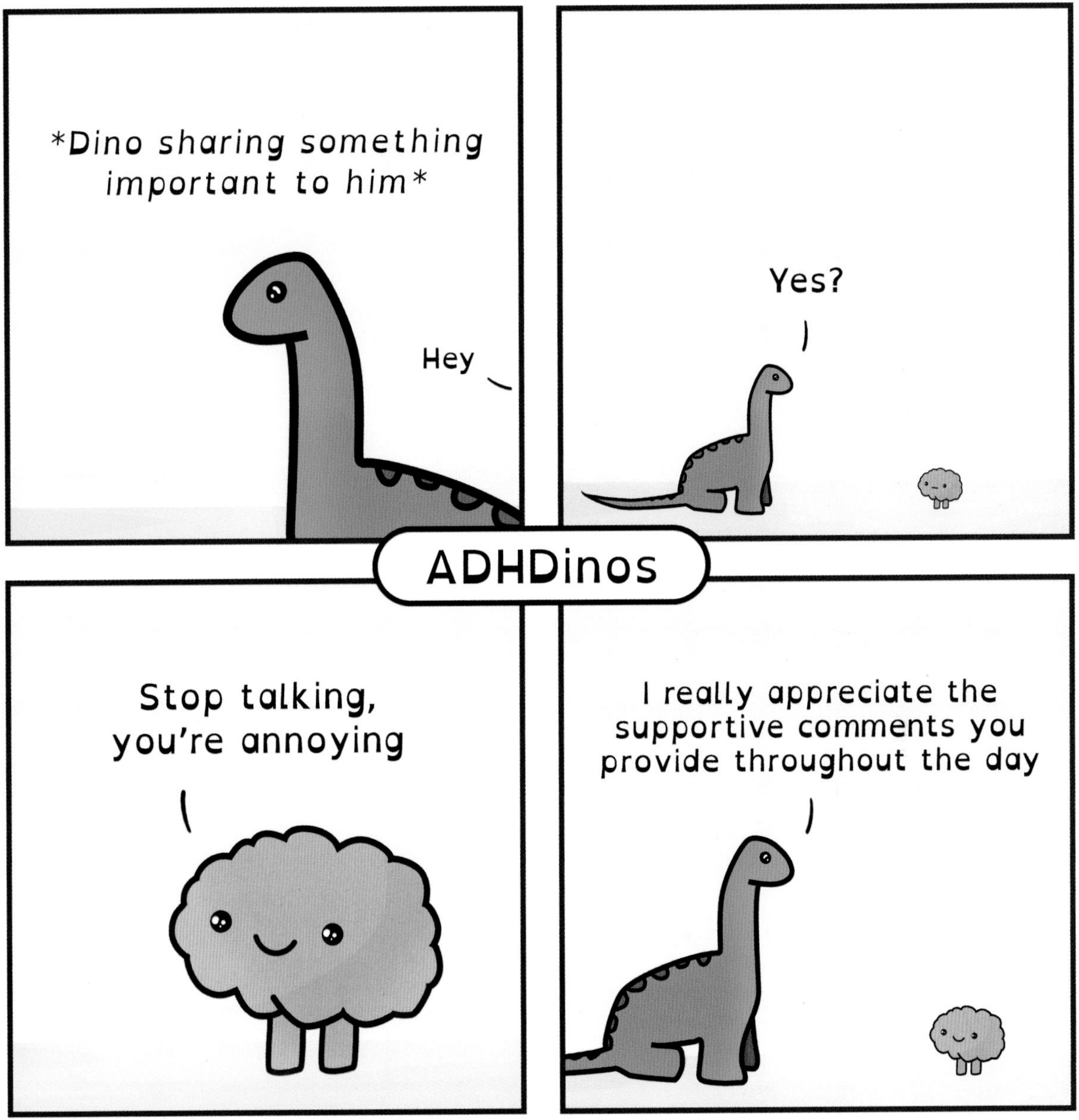
Dino sharing something important to him
Hey
Yes?
ADHDinos
Stop talking, you're annoying
I really appreciate the supportive comments you provide throughout the day

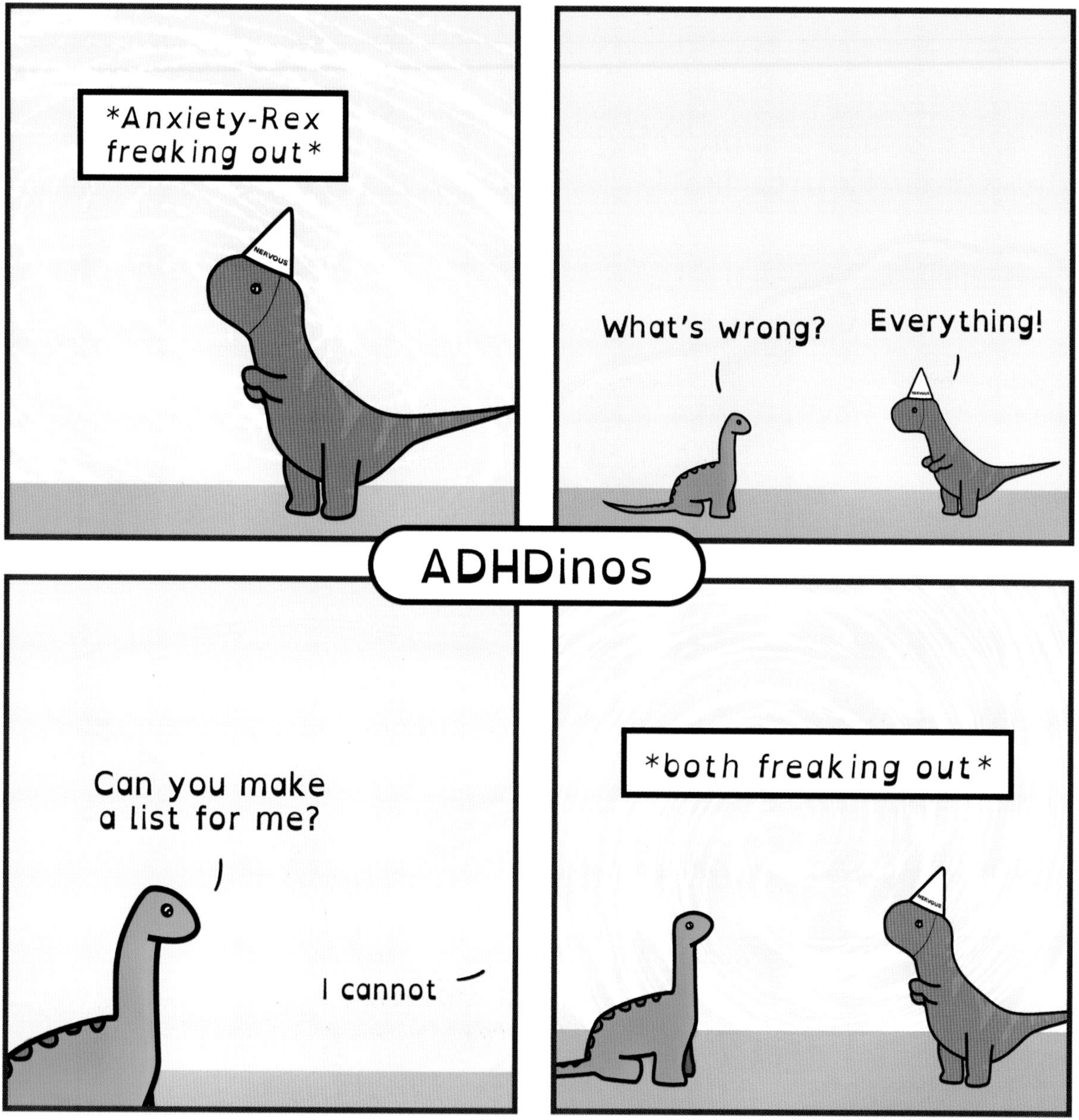
Anxiety-Rex freaking out
NERVOUS
What's wrong?
Everything!
ADHDinos
Can you make a list for me?
I cannot
both freaking out

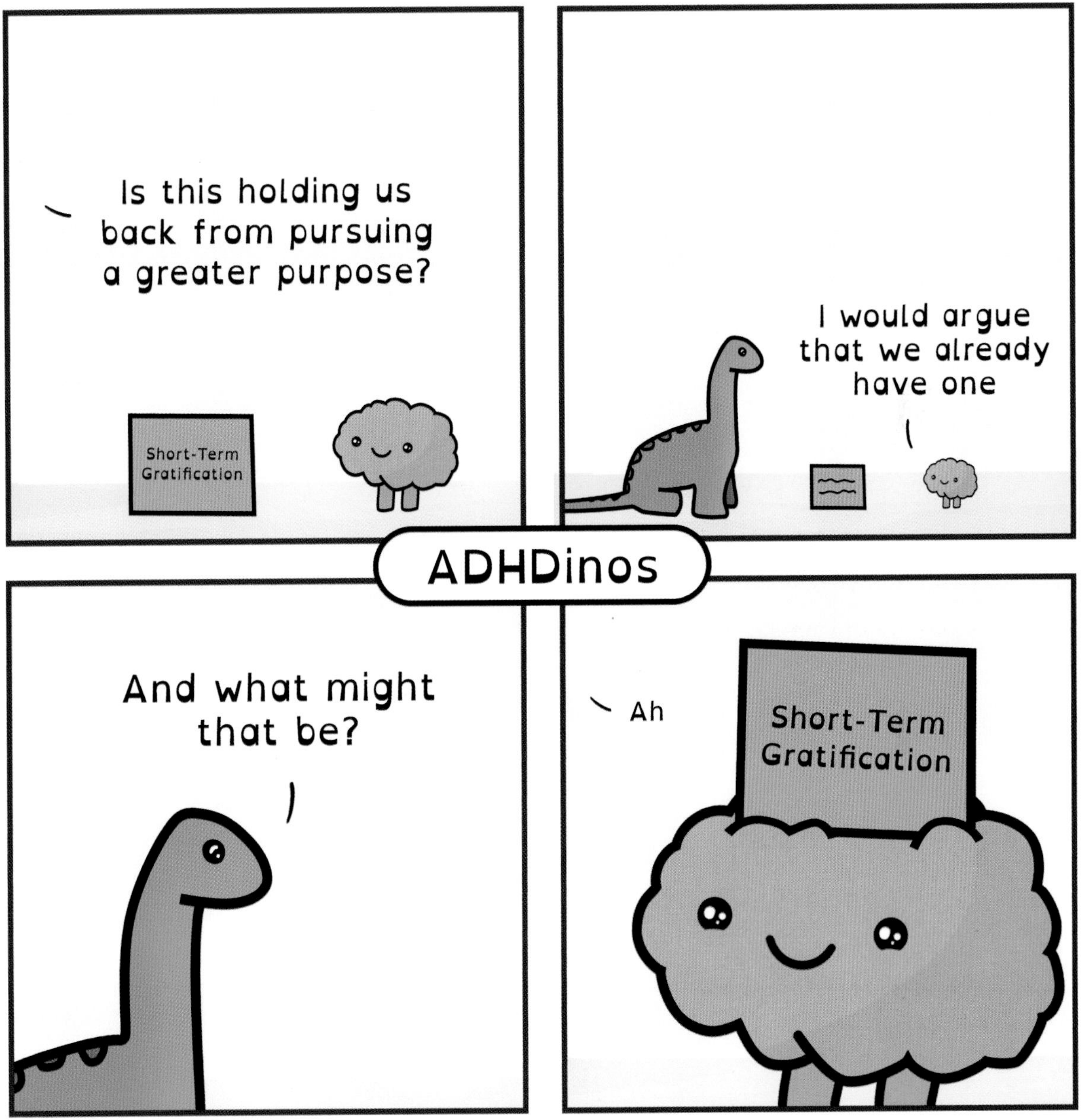
Is this holding us back from pursuing a greater purpose?
Short-Term Gratification
I would argue that we already have one
ADHDinos
And what might that be?
Ah
Short-Term Gratification

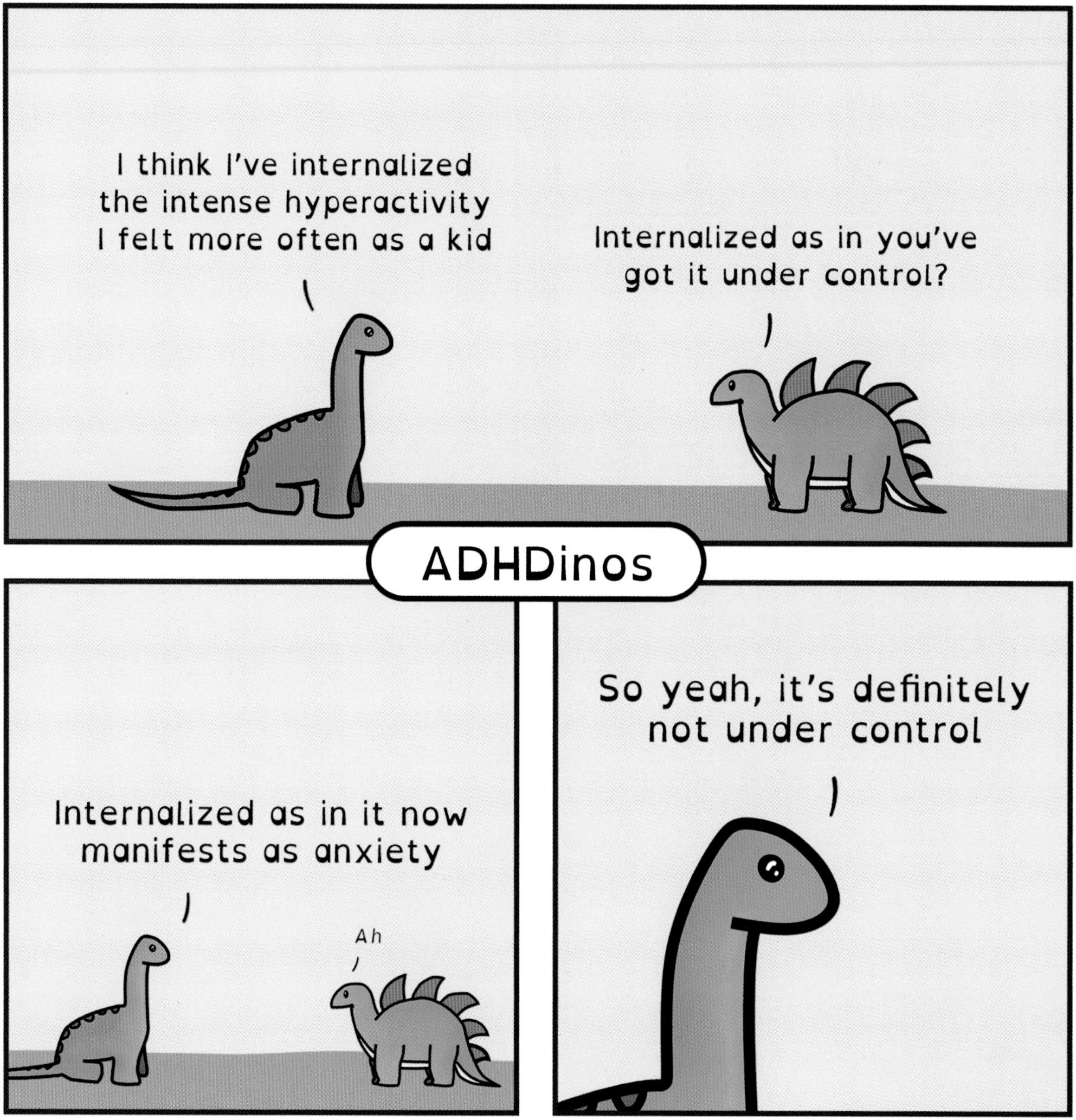
I think I've internalized the intense hyperactivity I felt more often as a kid
Internalized as in you've got it under control?
ADHDinos
Internalized as in it now manifests as anxiety
Ah
So yeah, it's definitely not under control

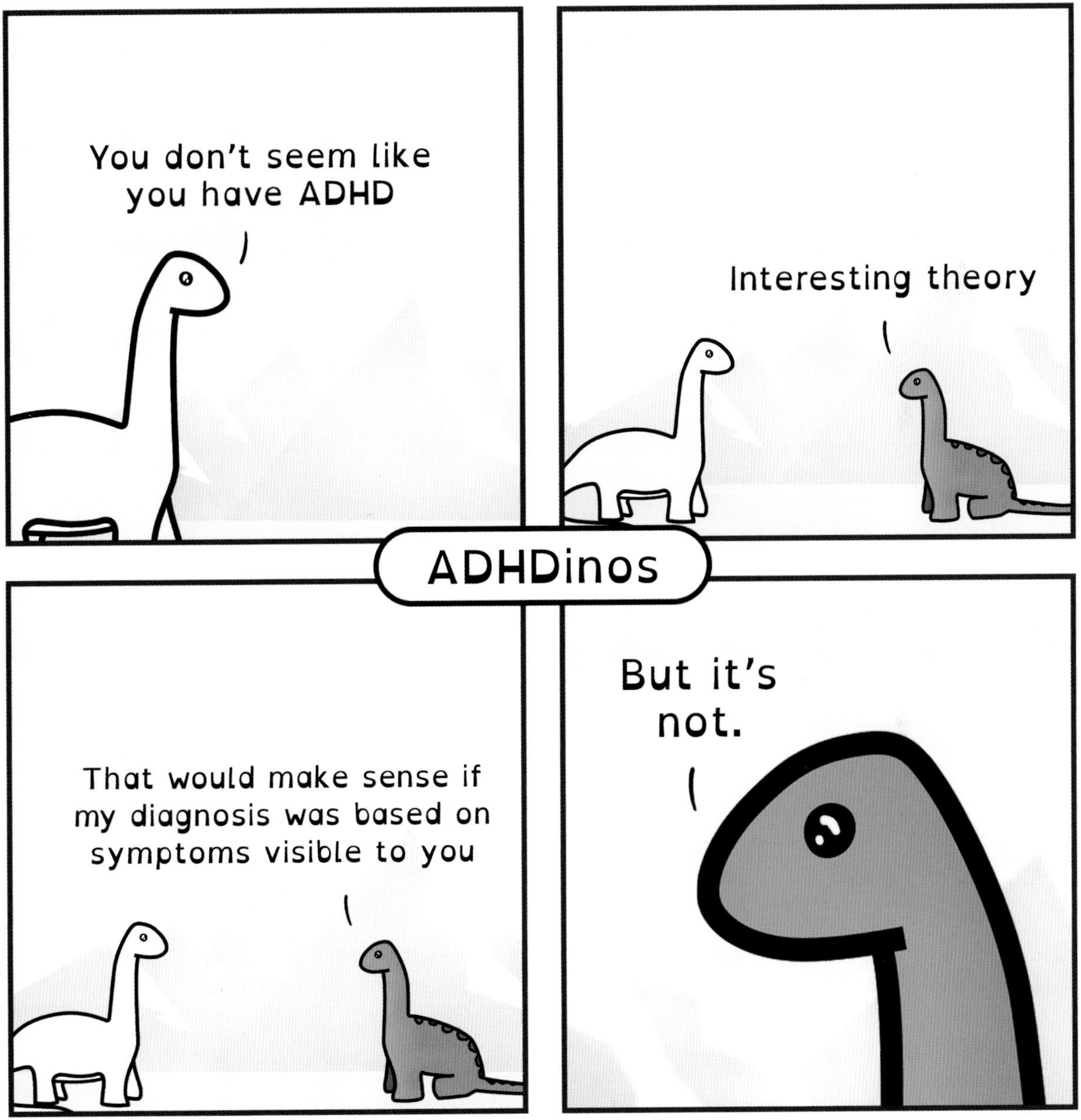
You don't seem like you have ADHD
Interesting theory
ADHDinos
That would make sense if my diagnosis was based on symptoms visible to you
But it's not.

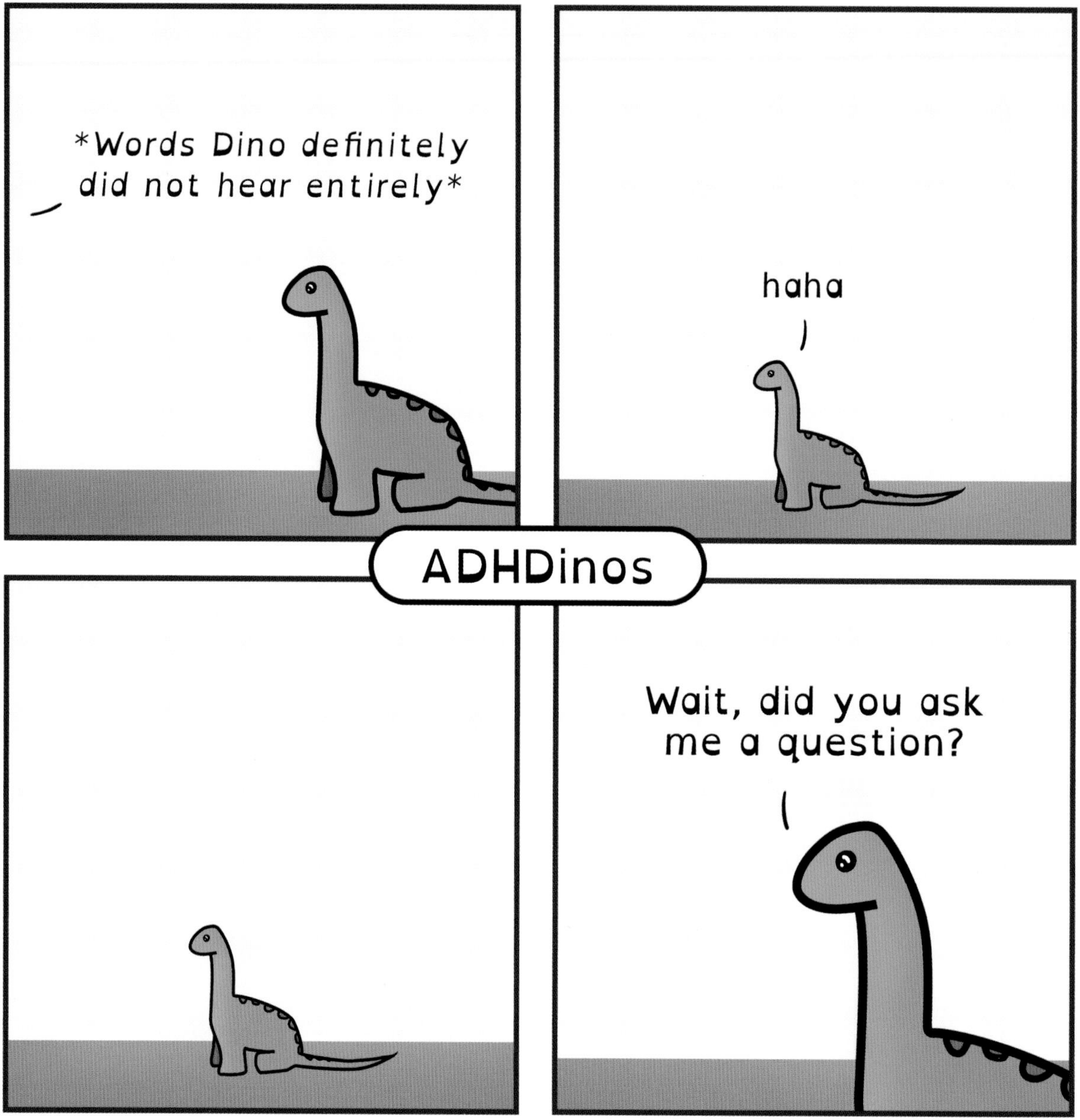
Words Dino definitely did not hear entirely
haha
ADHDinos
Wait, did you ask me a question?

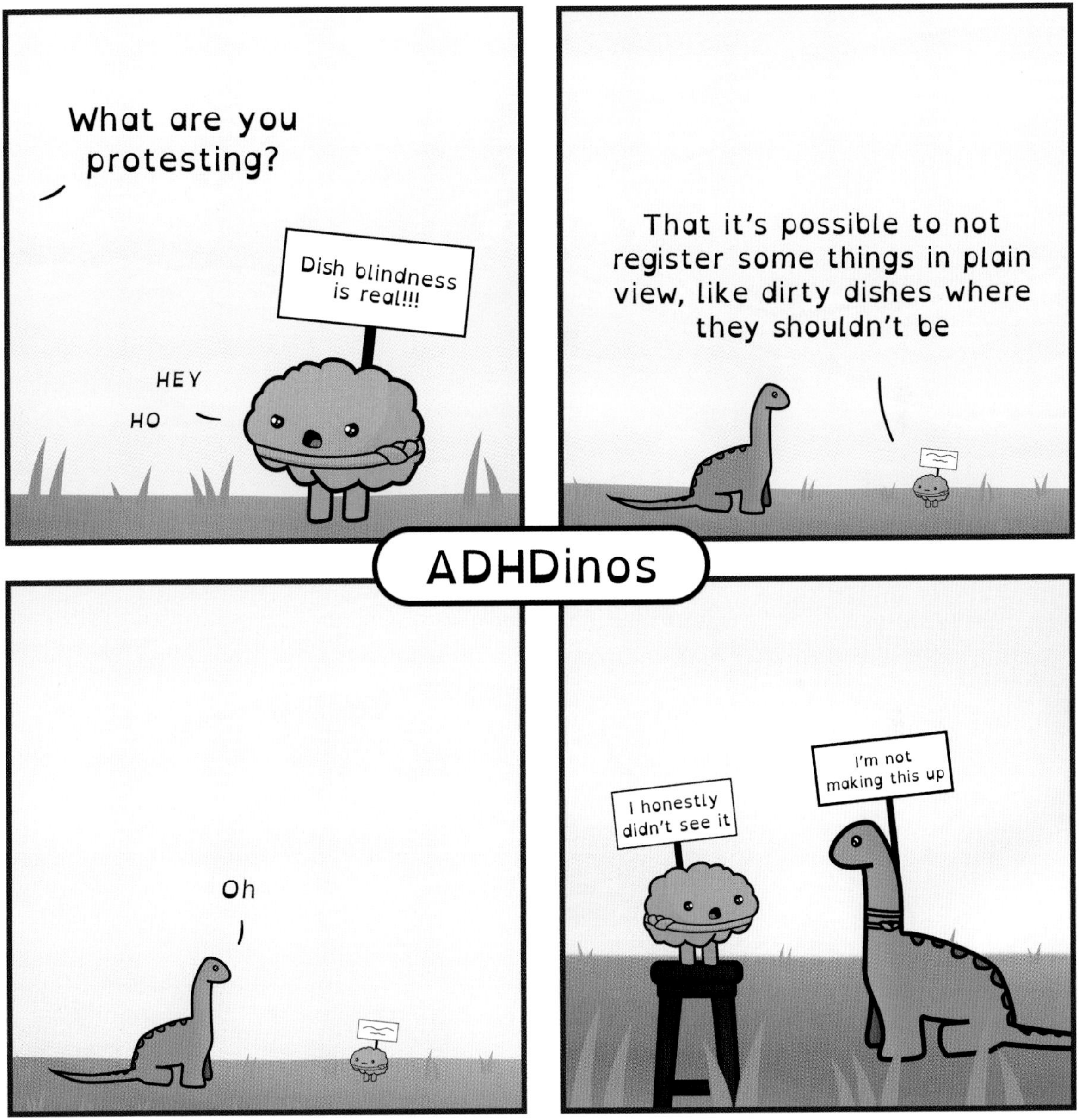
What are you protesting?
Dish blindness is real!!!
HEY
HO
That it's possible to not register some things in plain view, like dirty dishes where they shouldn't be
ADHDinos
Oh
I honestly didn't see it
I'm not making this up

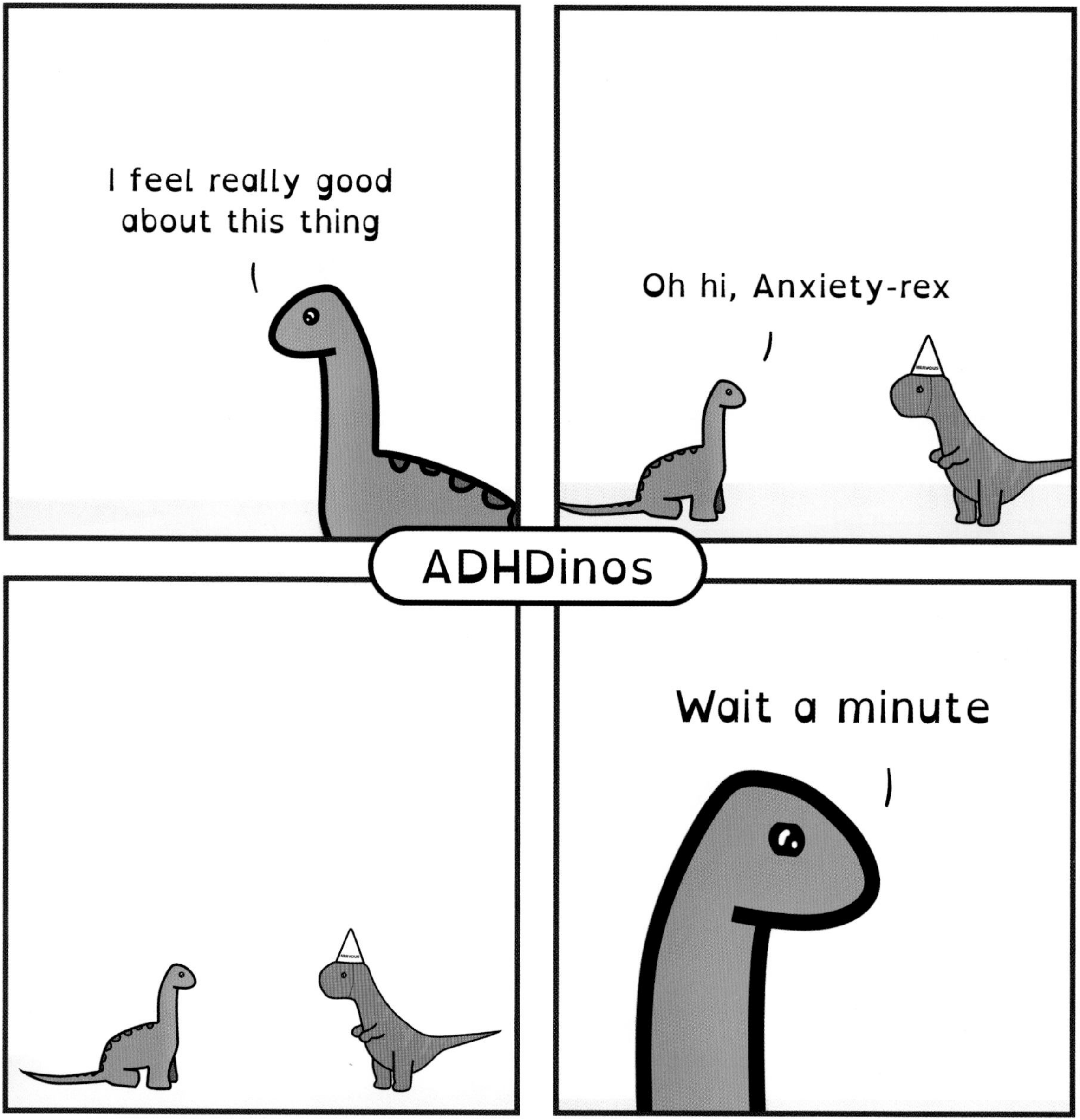
I feel really good about this thing
Oh hi, Anxiety-rex
ADHDinos
Wait a minute

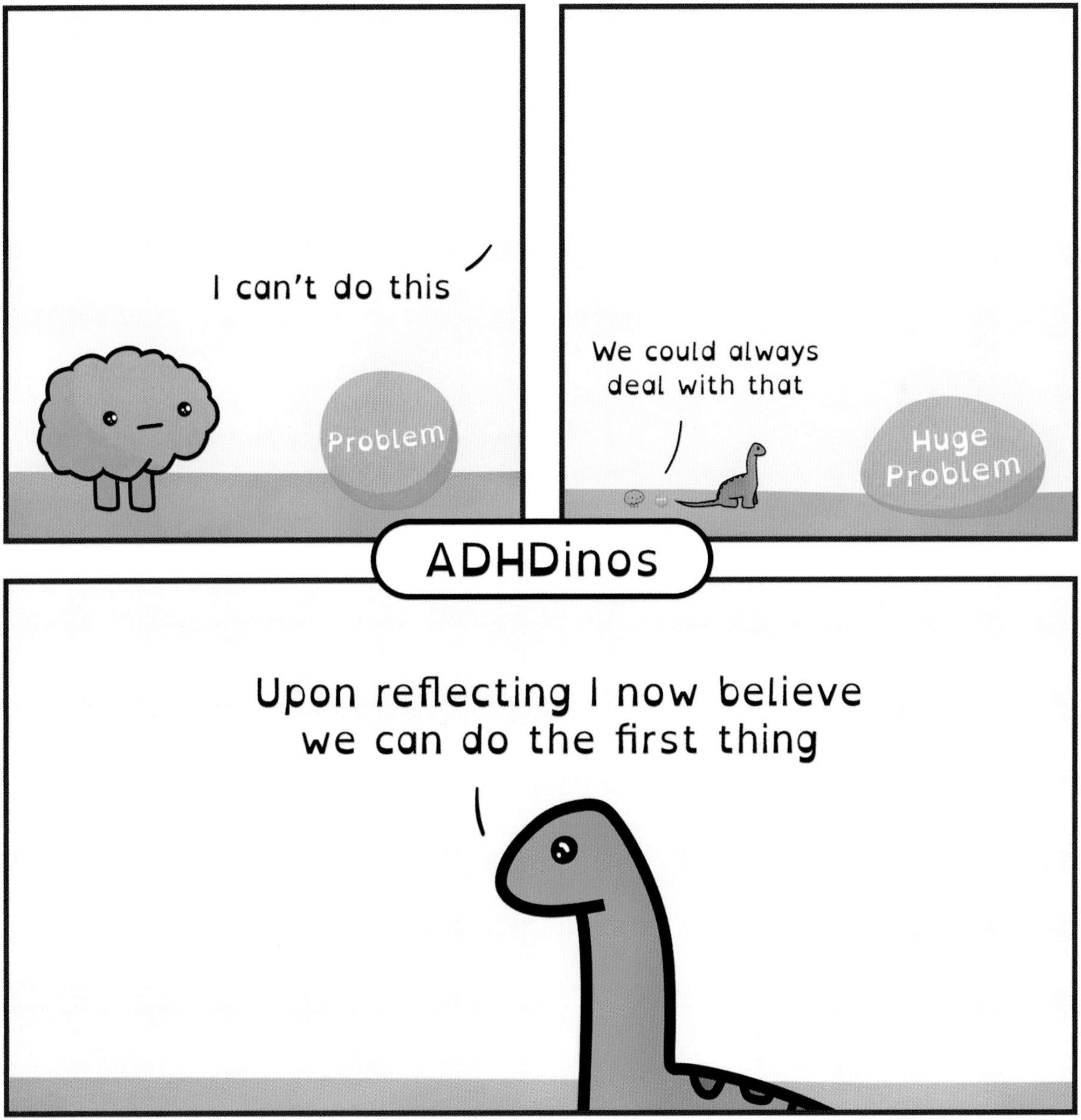
I can't do this
Problem
We could always deal with that
Huge Problem
ADHDinos
Upon reflecting I now believe we can do the first thing

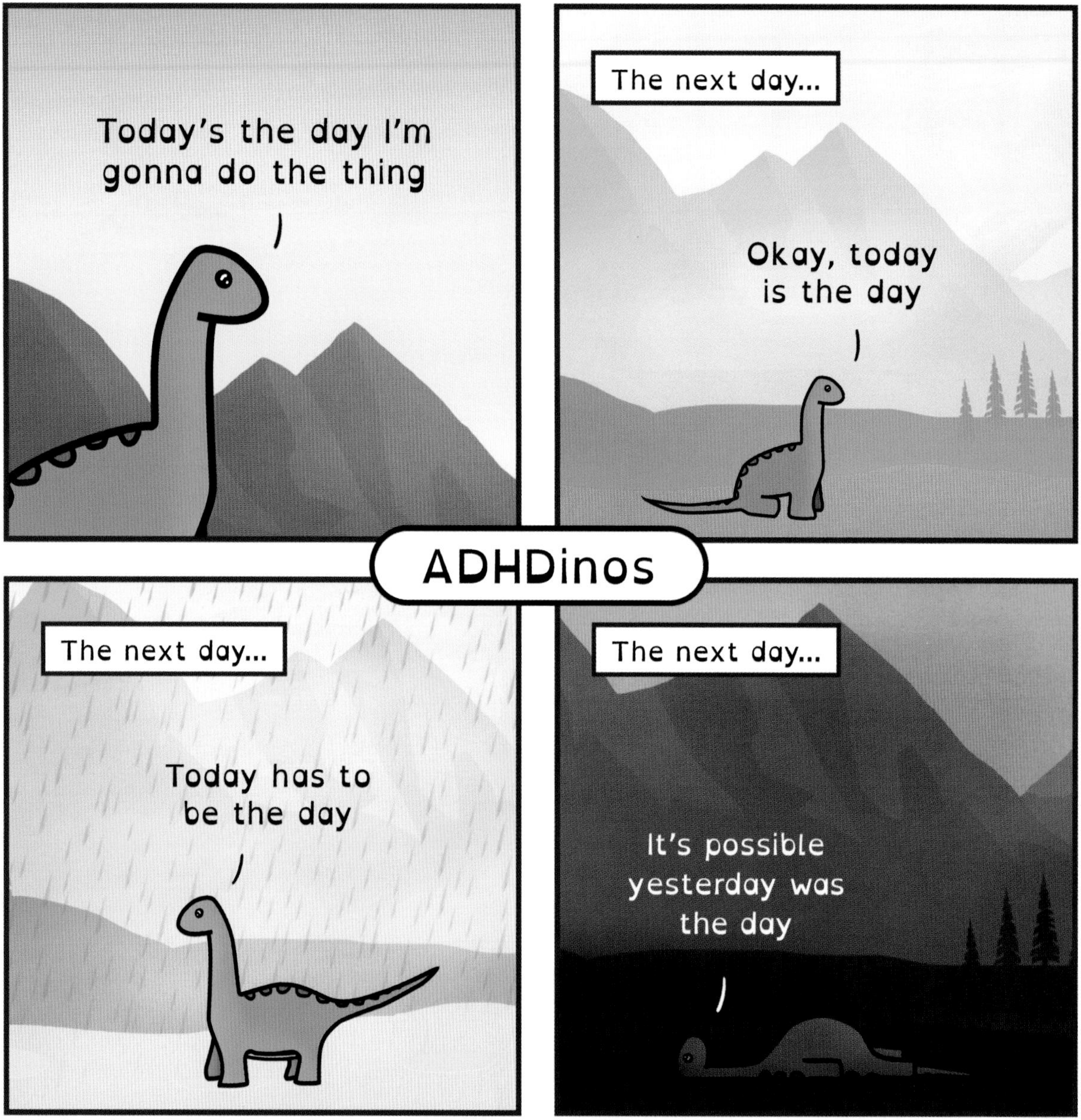
Today's the day I'm gonna do the thing
The next day...
Okay, today is the day
ADHDinos
The next day...
Today has to be the day
The next day...
It's possible yesterday was the day

Hyperfixation

Dino grew up thinking everyone hyperfixated as often as he did, and that it was perfectly normal to frequently stay up until the early hours of the morning researching a newly sparked passion or to spend unspeakable amounts of money on prospective hobbies. While hyperfixating isn't exclusive to individuals with ADHD, they experience it far more frequently and intensely than those who don't have ADHD.[*]

Hyperfixation can be an amazing tool to do a lot in a short amount of time, but it can become a problem when hyperfixating on the wrong thing, or when interest in a hyperfixation declines just as quickly as it arose (let's not start on abandoned hobbies). Hyperfixation can also permanently disrupt routines, which Dino struggles quite a lot in establishing.

[*] Ashinoff, B.K., & Abu-Akel, A. Hyperfocus: the forgotten frontier of attention. *Psychological Research* 85, 1–19 (2021). https://doi.org/10.1007/s00426-019-01245-8

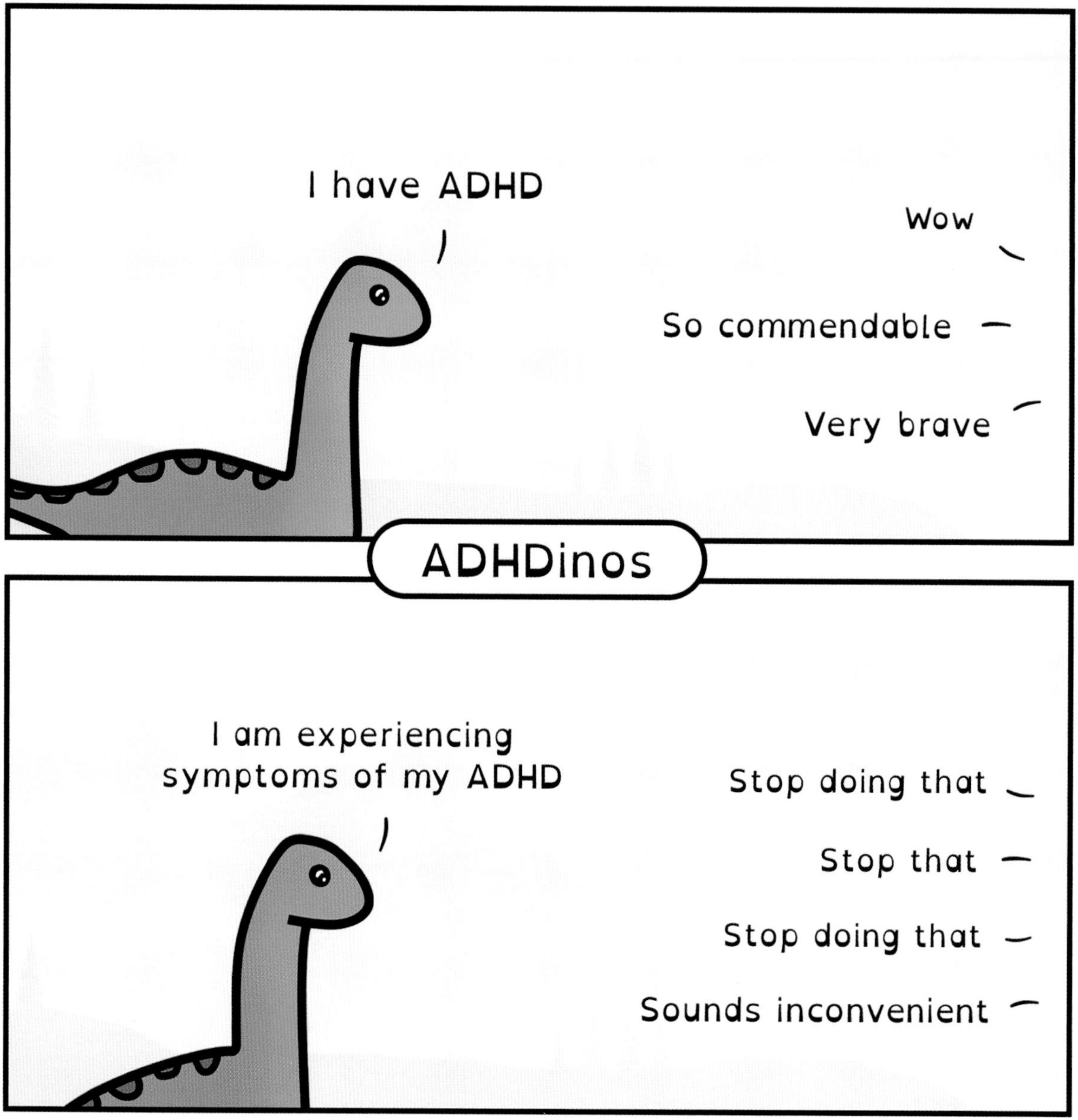
I have ADHD
Wow
So commendable
Very brave
ADHDinos
I am experiencing symptoms of my ADHD
Stop doing that
Stop that
Stop doing that
Sounds inconvenient

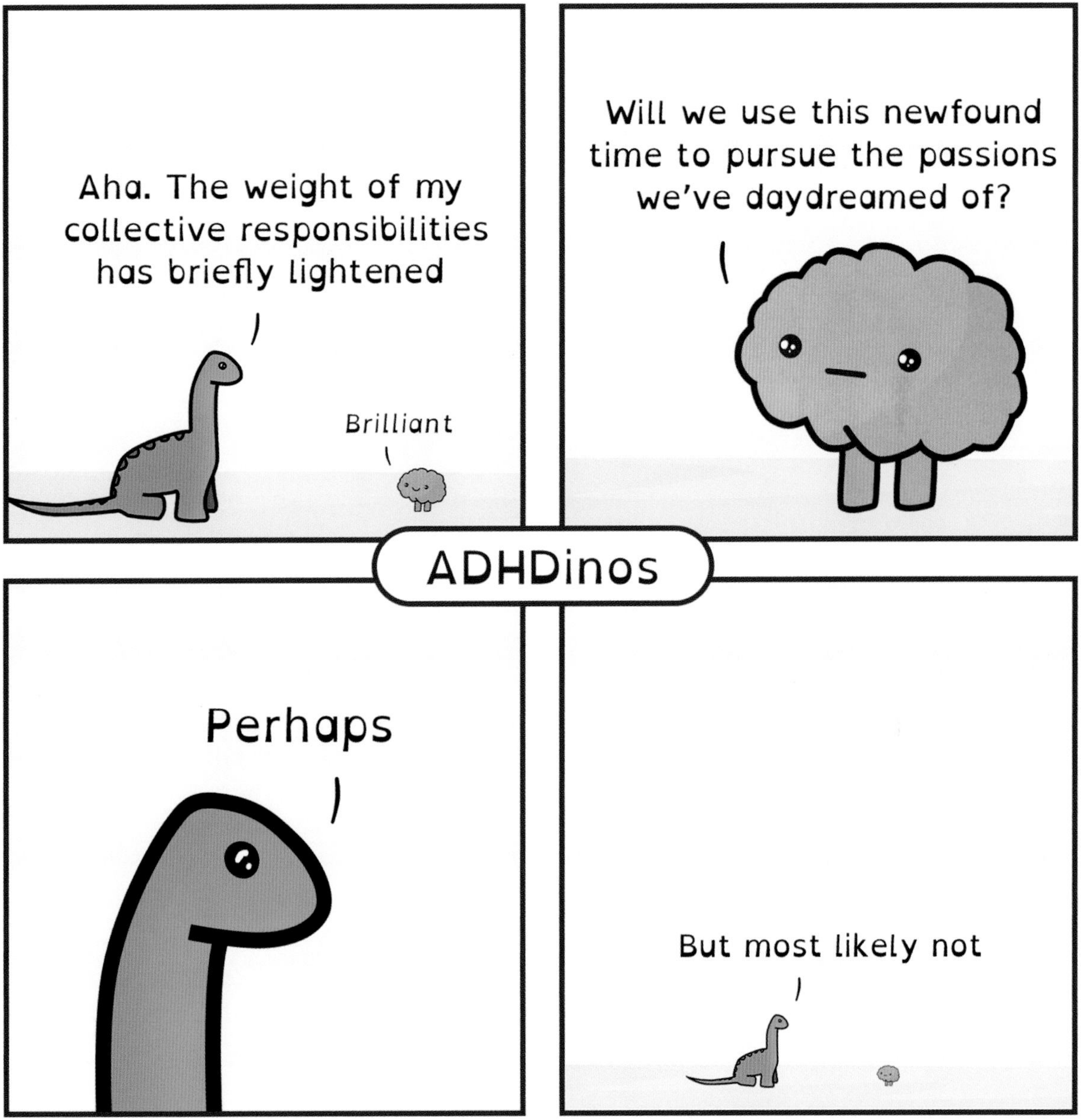
Aha. The weight of my collective responsibilities has briefly lightened
Brilliant
Will we use this newfound time to pursue the passions we've daydreamed of?
ADHDinos
Perhaps
But most likely not

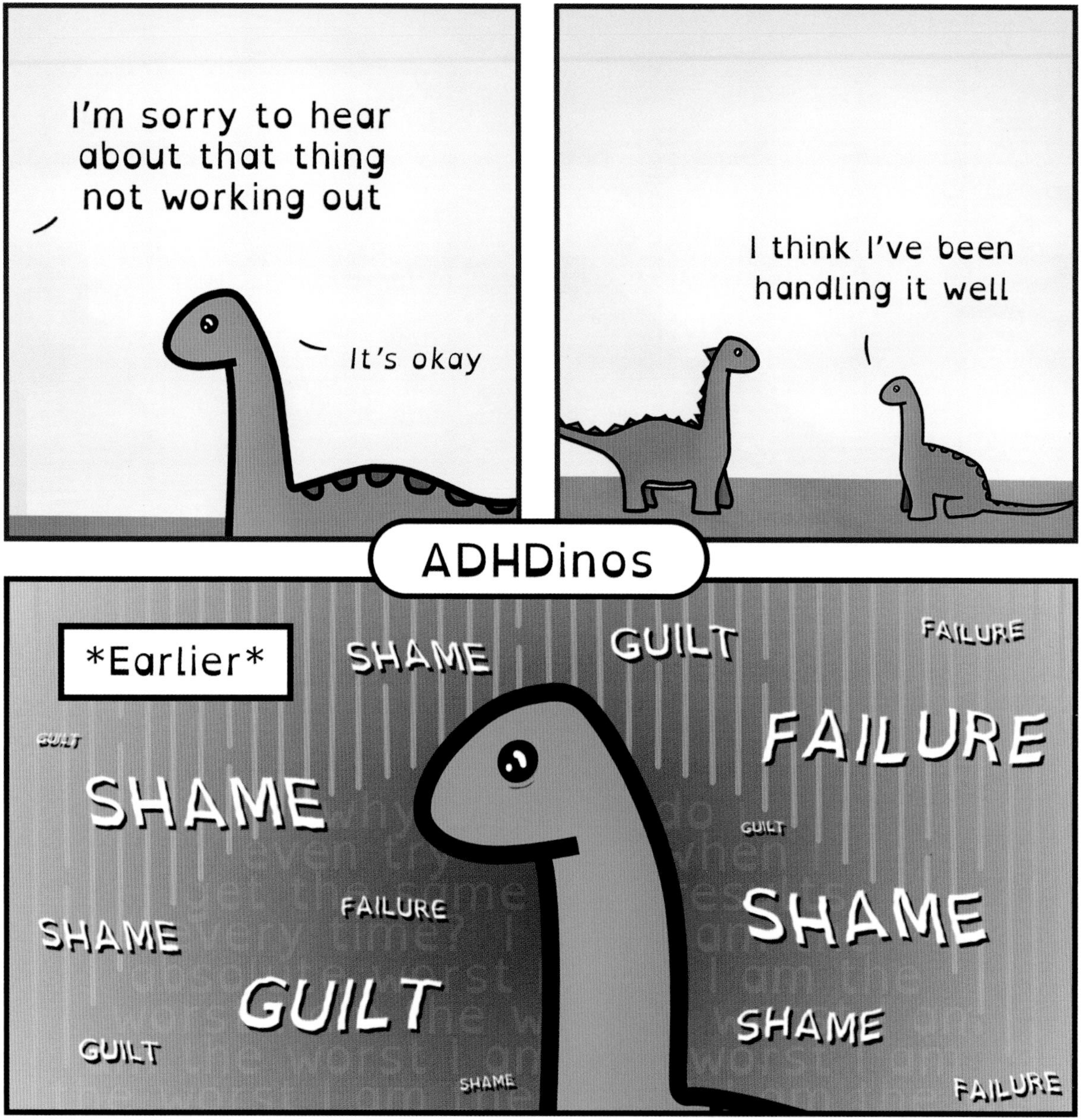
I'm sorry to hear about that thing not working out
It's okay
I think I've been handling it well
ADHDinos
Earlier
SHAME
GUILT
FAILURE
GUILT
SHAME
FAILURE
GUILT
FAILURE
SHAME
SHAME
SHAME
GUILT
SHAME
GUILT
SHAME
FAILURE

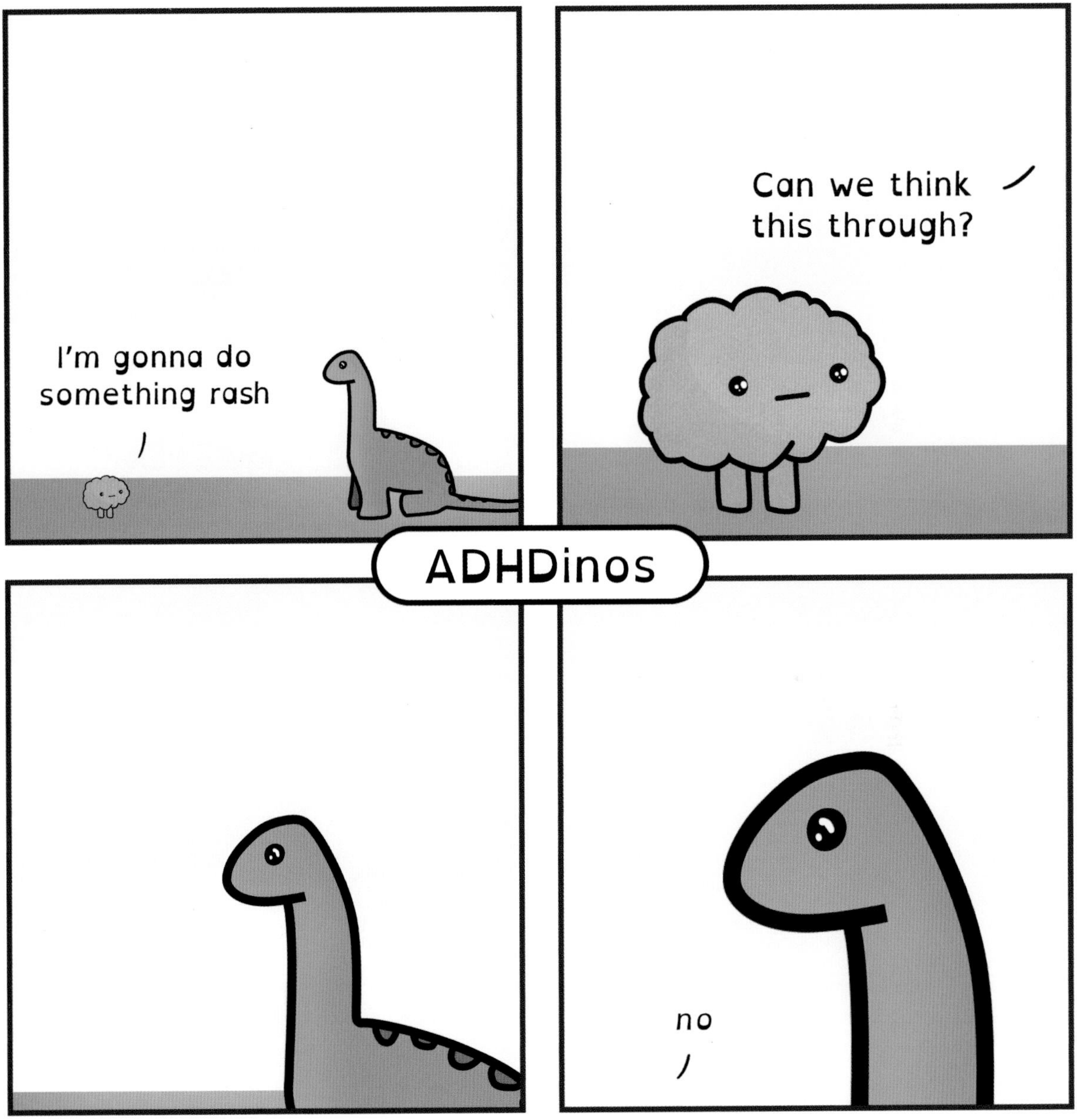
I'm gonna do something rash
Can we think this through?
ADHDinos
no

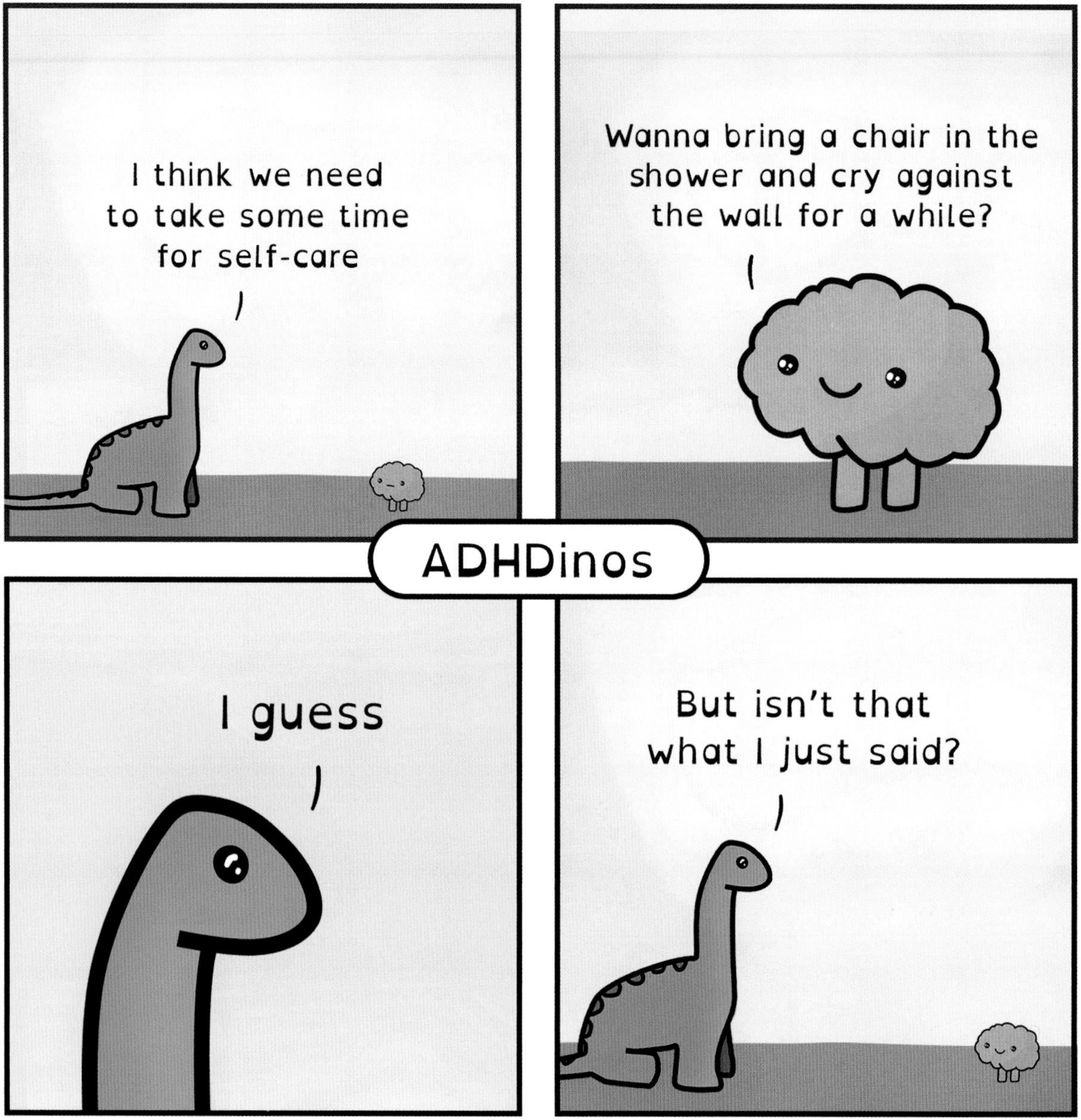
I think we need to take some time for self-care
Wanna bring a chair in the shower and cry against the wall for a while?
ADHDinos
I guess
But isn't that what I just said?

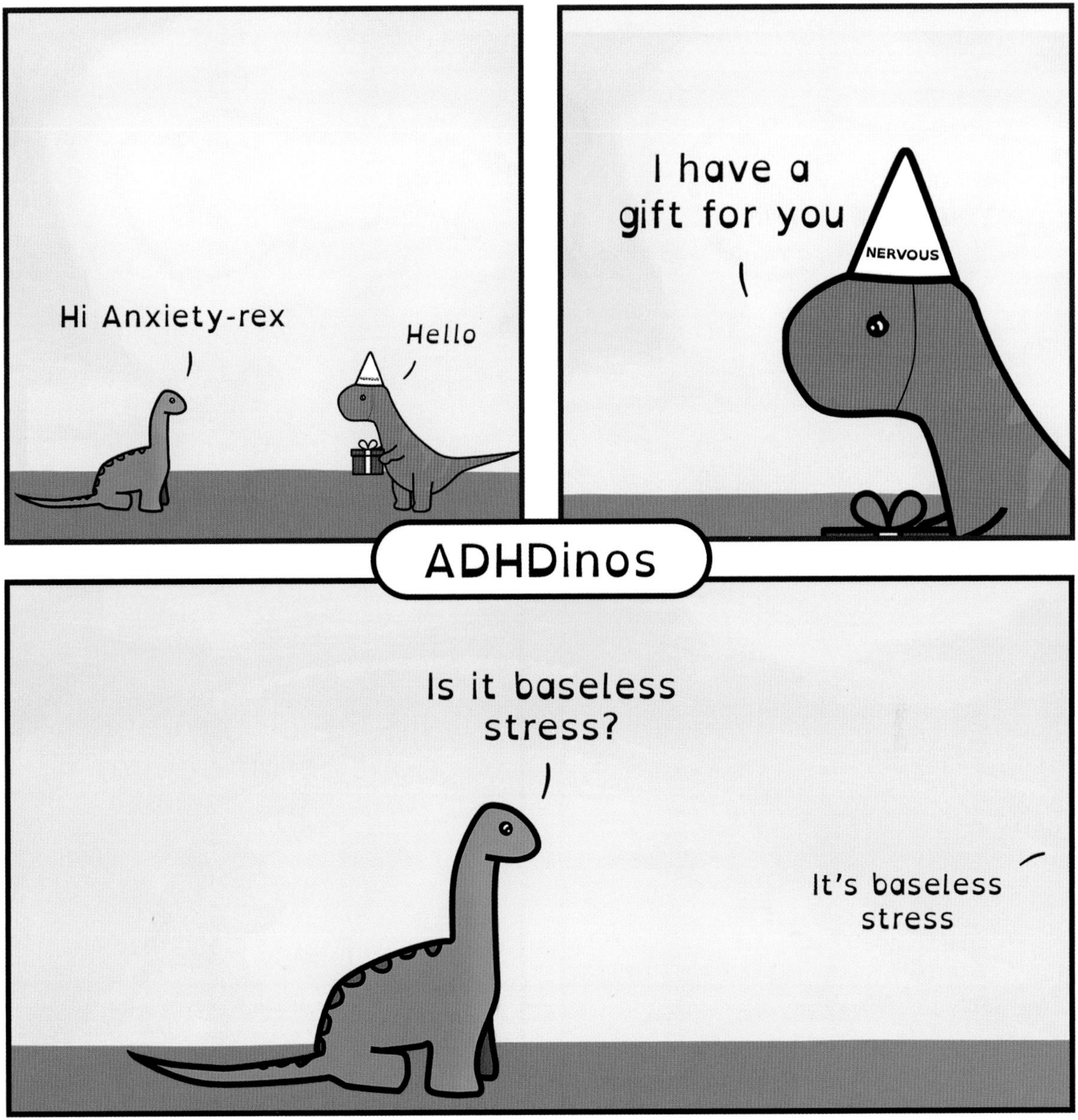
Hi Anxiety-rex
Hello
NERVOUS
I have a gift for you
NERVOUS
ADHDinos
Is it baseless stress?
It's baseless stress

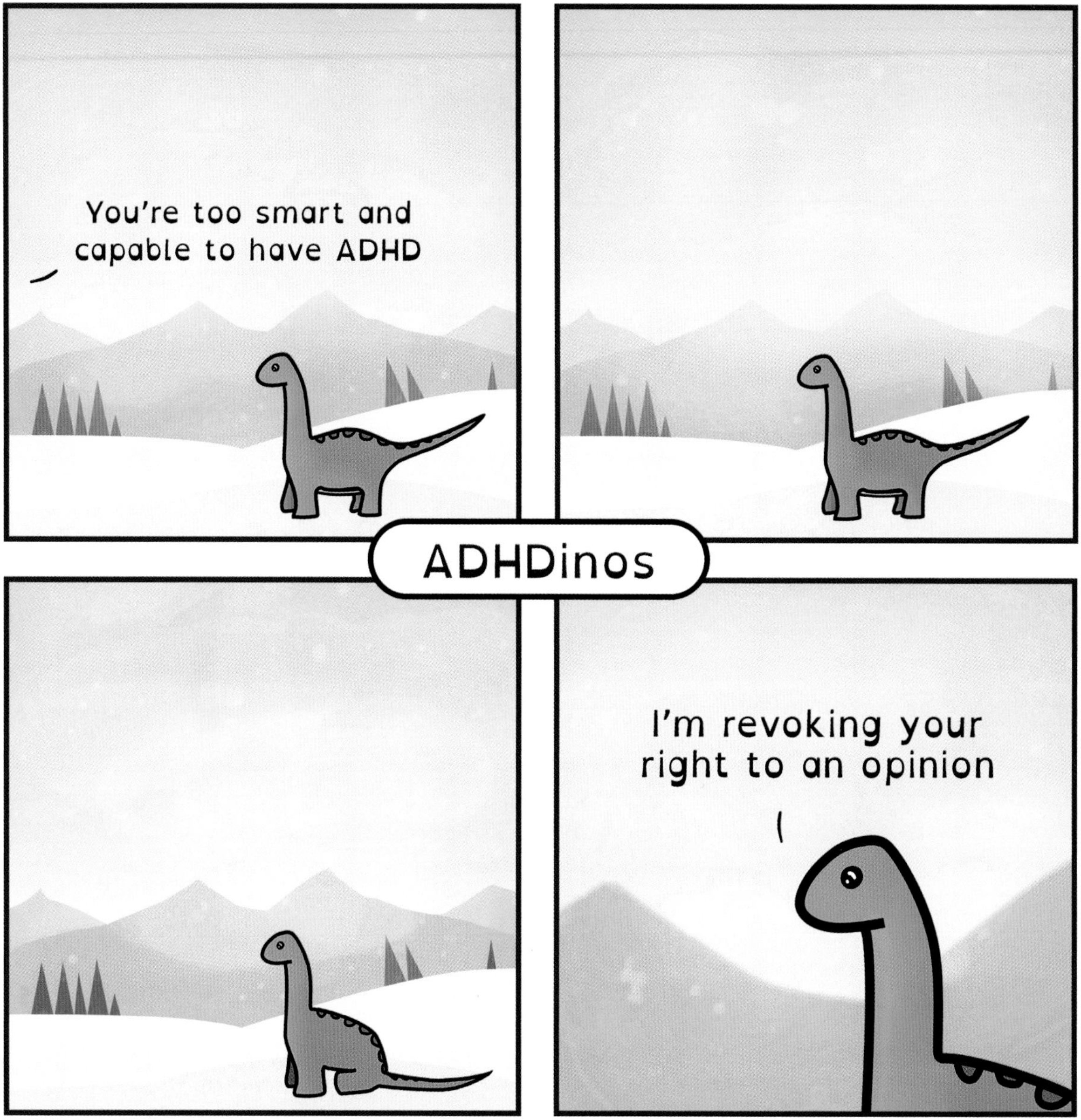
You're too smart and capable to have ADHD
ADHDinos
I'm revoking your right to an opinion

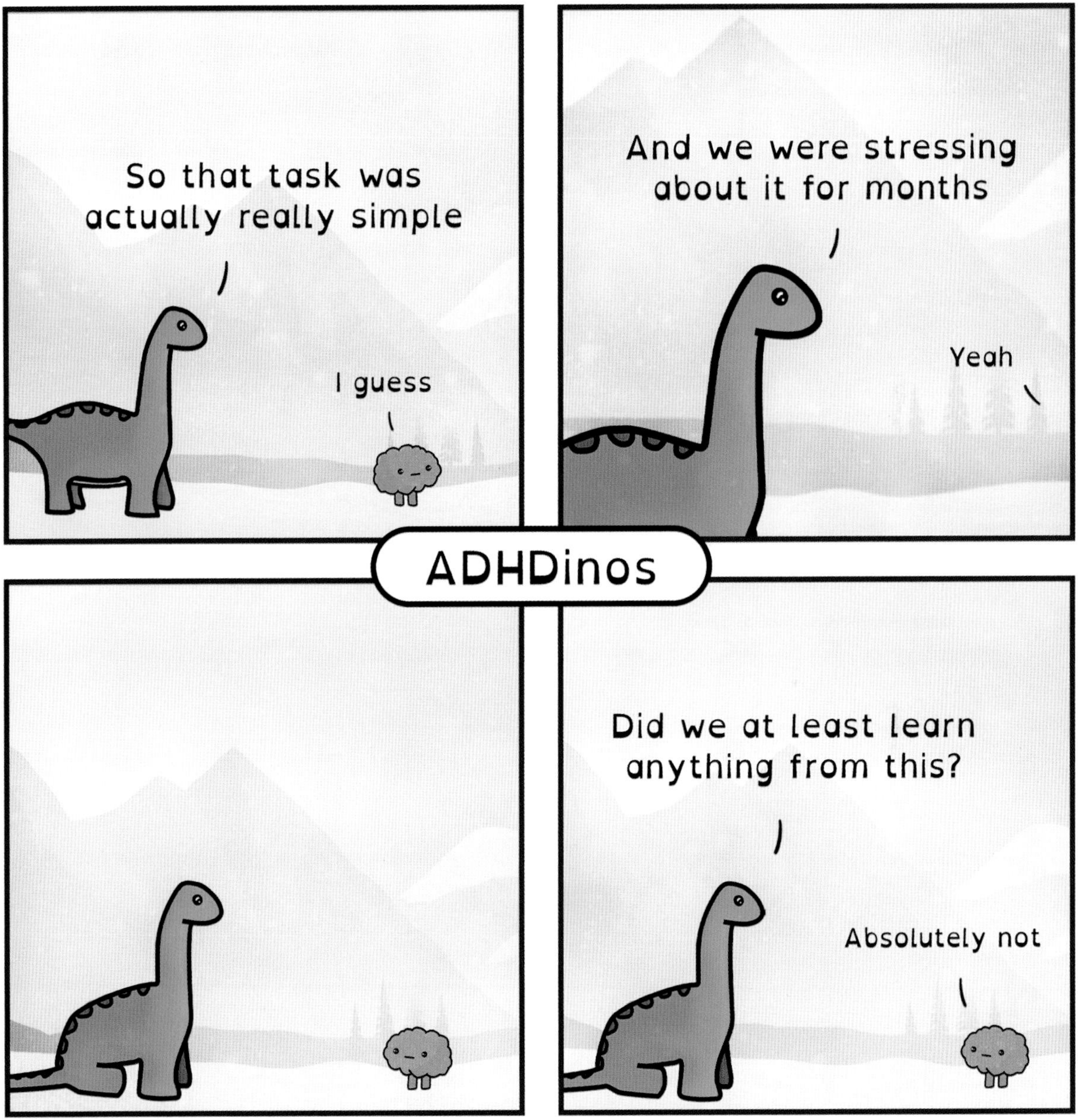
So that task was actually really simple
I guess
And we were stressing about it for months
Yeah
ADHDinos
Did we at least learn anything from this?
Absolutely not

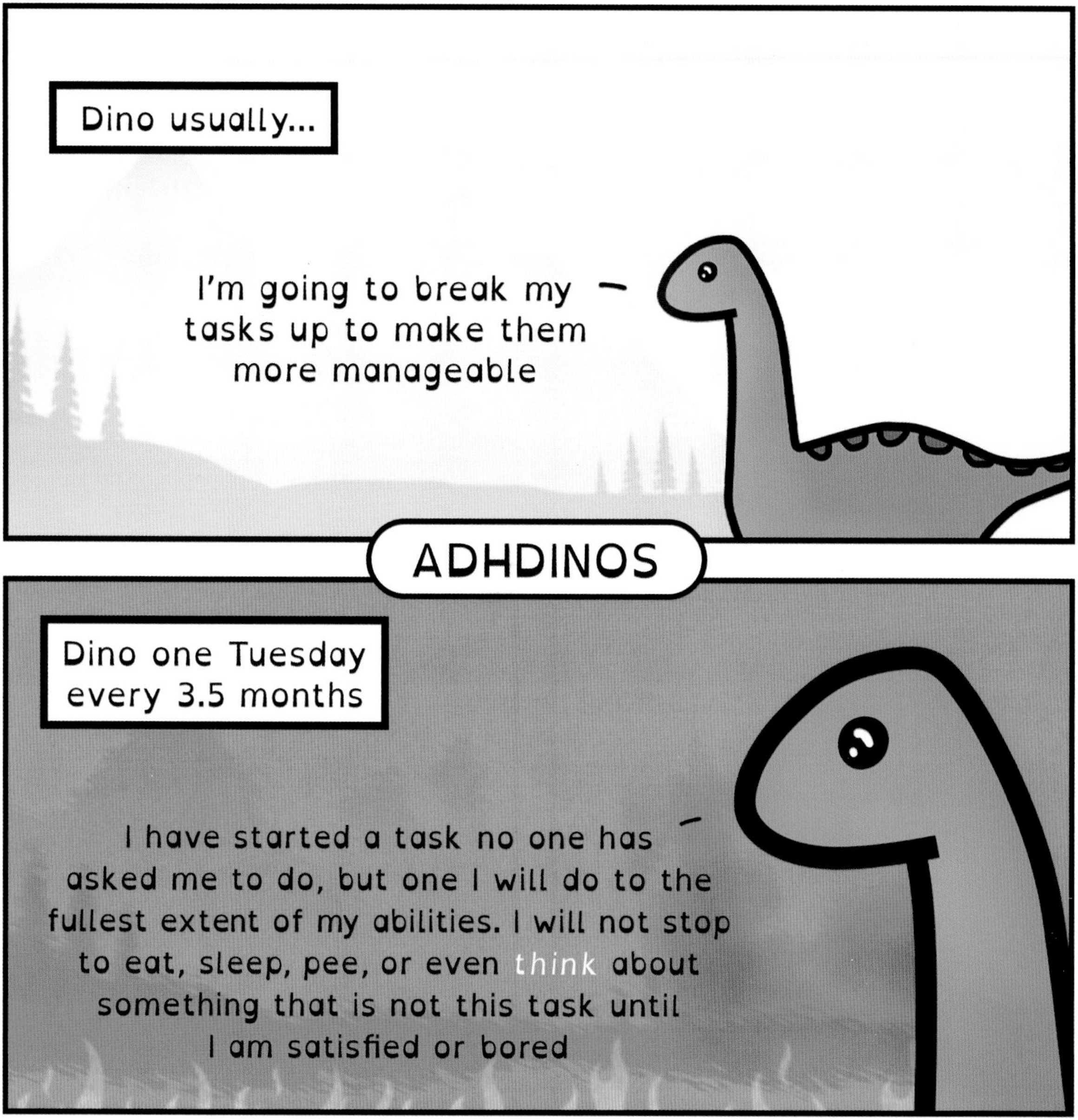
Dino usually...
I'm going to break my tasks up to make them more manageable
ADHDINOS
Dino one Tuesday every 3.5 months
I have started a task no one has asked me to do, but one I will do to the fullest extent of my abilities. I will not stop to eat, sleep, pee, or even think about something that is not this task until I am satisfied or bored

Hobbies

Every so often, Dino finds himself enamored with a new hobby. Tens (sometimes hundreds) of hours will subsequently be spent reading, learning, planning, and obsessing over it.

When Dino focuses on things he enjoys or is good at, he will develop reliable skills in these areas. But admittedly, he tends to neglect things he finds difficult, which can leave some big holes in his knowledge. This makes it much harder for him to rely on his skills and often leads to being criticized for "preventable" mistakes, undermining his confidence and passion.

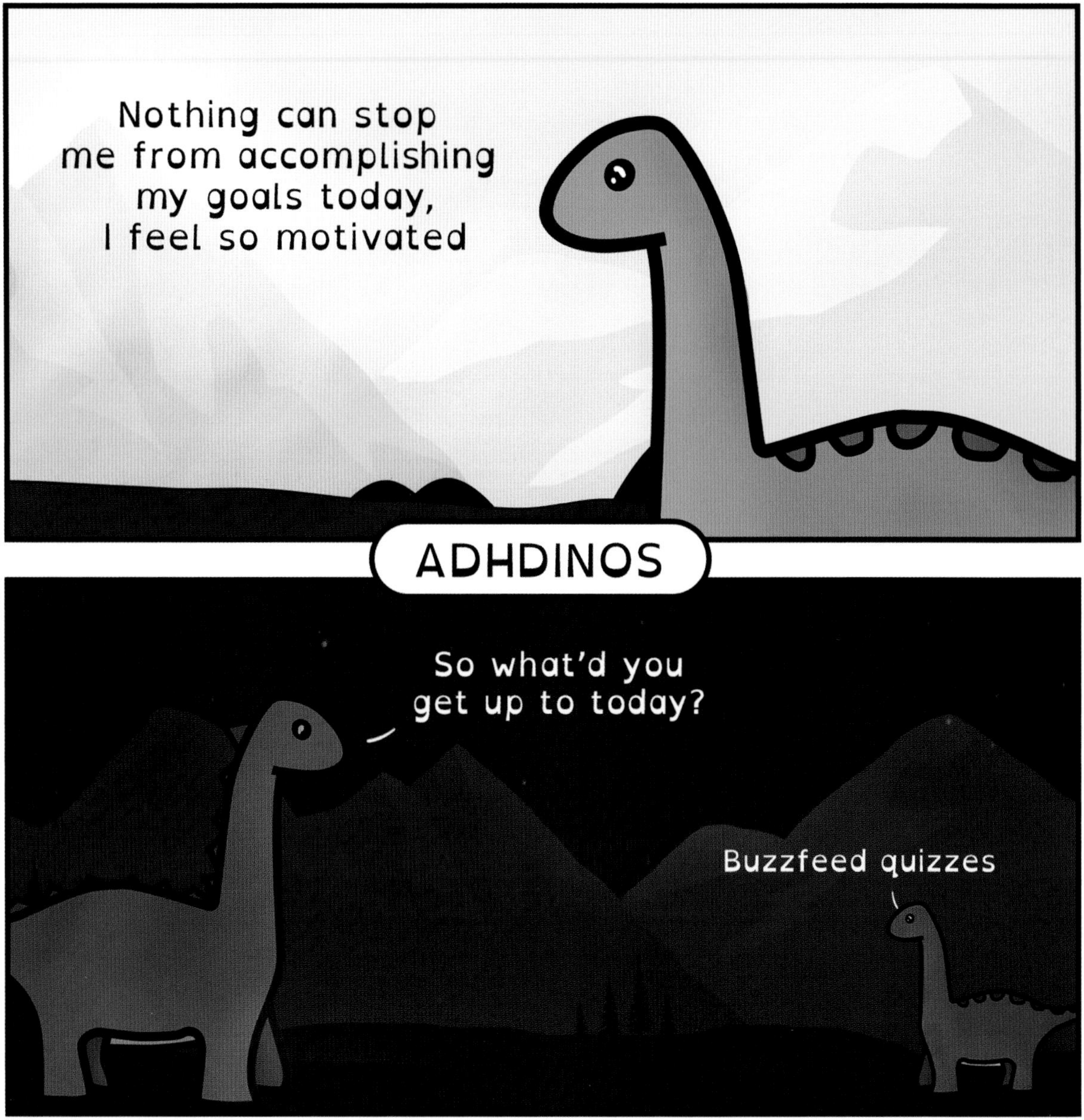

Nothing can stop me from accomplishing my goals today, I feel so motivated
ADHDINOS
So what'd you get up to today?
Buzzfeed quizzes

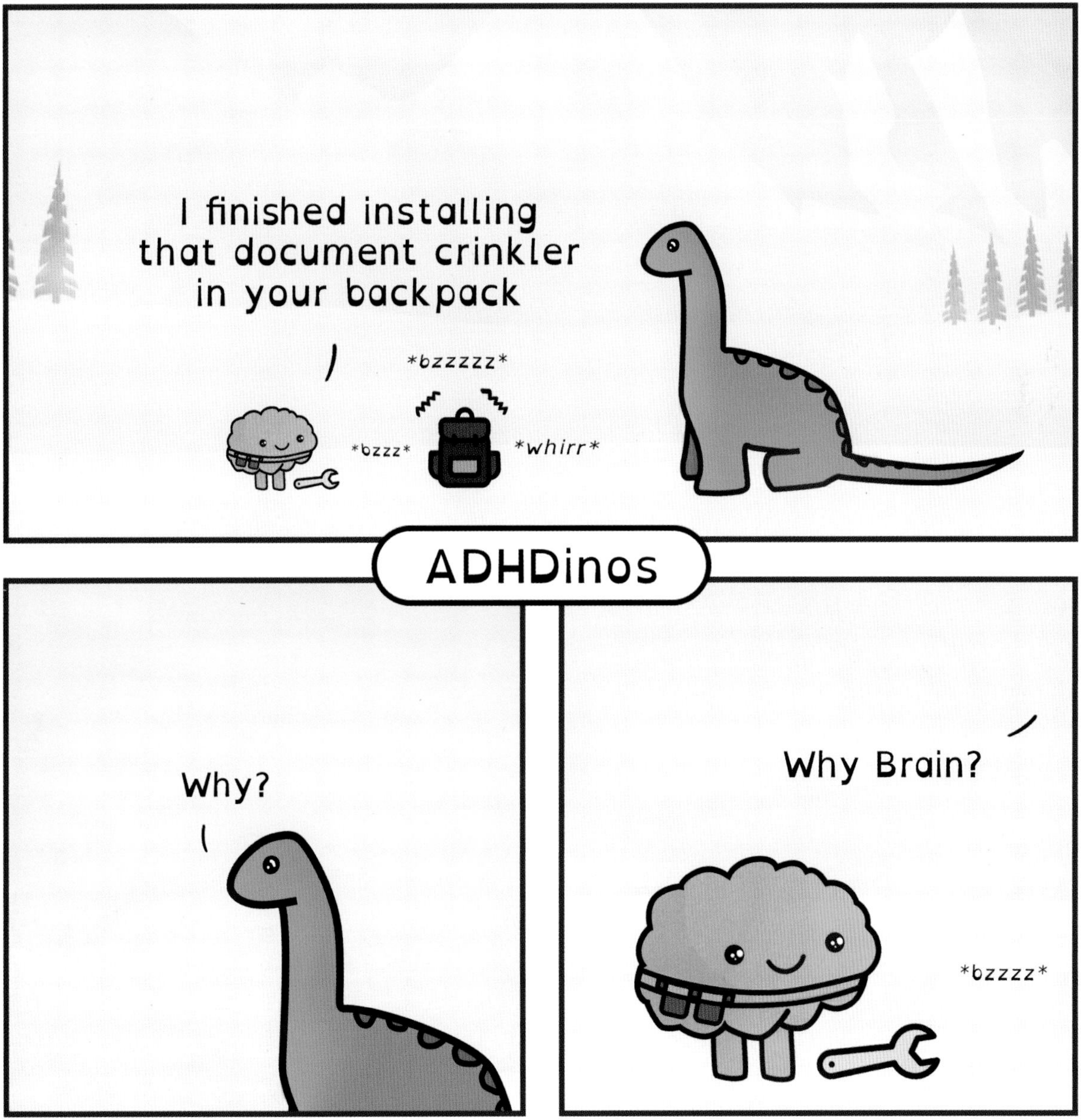
I finished installing that document crinkler in your backpack
bzzzzz
bzzz
whirr
ADHDinos
Why?
Why Brain?
bzzzz

Glossary

ADHD: Attention deficit hyperactivity disorder is a complex neurological condition that often impacts an individual's organization, focus, and impulse control. Both adults and children can have ADHD.

Anxiety: Anxiety is a standard response to stressors. Visible signs of anxiety can include an increased heart rate, sweating, and rapid breathing, but it can also manifest internally/in one's head. Everyone experiences anxiety differently and to vastly varying degrees, but excessive anxiety can hinder one's ability to function day-to-day.

Burnout: Burnout is a state of mental, physical, and emotional exhaustion resulting from pushing oneself too hard, for too long. Signs of burnout can include anxiety, detachment, lack of sleep, and lack of motivation.

Emotional Dysregulation: Emotional dysregulation refers to an inability to control one's emotional response to situations, often resulting in overblown reactions to easily fixable issues.

Executive Dysfunction: Executive dysfunction represents a struggle to control one's thoughts, emotions, and behaviors—often referred to as executive functions.

Executive Functions: Executive functions are a set of cognitive abilities involved in behavior control. They can include self-control, flexibility, task initiation, organization, working memory, emotional regulation, time management, and focus.

Hyperfocus: Plainly, hyperfocus is excessive, undivided attention on one thing for an extended period of time. Someone can hyperfocus on almost anything, ranging from hobbies to movies to people. Hyperfocus can be a great tool for accomplishing a lot in a short amount of time, but it can also cause major disruptions in routine responsibilities.

Negative Self-Talk: Negative self-talk refers to a persistent and overly critical inner dialogue that undermines one's abilities and self-confidence.

Neurodivergent: An individual with atypical cognition. They may have different strengths and face different challenges than their peers. This term can be used to describe those with autism, ADHD, and dyslexia, to name a few.

Neurotypical: An individual with typical neurological development.

Self-Control: Self-control refers to one's ability to inhibit impulse and control their actions in the pursuit of long-term goals.

Self-Regulation: The ability to identify causes of problematic impulses and to be willing to learn how to reduce their frequency/impact. Self-regulation is often confused with self-control.

Task Initiation: Individuals with ADHD often struggle with starting a task even when they wish or need to do so, regardless of consequences. The ability to take on a task is often referred to as task initiation.

Time Blindness: Time blindness refers to a general difficulty accurately assessing the passing of time or accurately allocating time for upcoming tasks. It often contributes to lateness and an inability to complete tasks on time.

Working Memory: This can be thought about as the "temporary storage" in one's brain required to manage multiple ideas or thoughts while performing an action. Individuals with ADHD frequently have a significant deficit in working memory compared to their neurotypical peers, contributing to forgetfulness and a difficulty managing multiple tasks simultaneously.

About the Author

Ryan Keats is a recent graduate of the University of Western Ontario with a background in social media, marketing, creative photography, and graphic design. Following his diagnosis of adult ADHD, he started drawing ADHDinos as a cathartic way to work through his symptoms and connect with others who deal with similar struggles.

Visit Ryan online and read his comics at:

 ADHDinos.com

 https://www.instagram.com/adhdinos/

 https://www.reddit.com/r/ADHDinos/